Hoods on the Hill

HOODS ON THE HILL

How Mulroney and His Gang Rammed the GST Past Parliament and Down Our Throats

Royce Frith

Coach House Press
Toronto

*Illustrations by Mallette (p. 14), by Cam (p. 22, 56) and by Zazulak (p. 72)
reprinted by kind permission of the artists. Illustration by MacPherson (p. 82)
reprinted with permission of The Toronto Star Syndicate. Illustration by Nease
(p. 94) reprinted with permission of The Southam Syndicate.*

Canadian Cataloguing in Publication Data
Frith, Royce, 1923-
Hoods on the Hill: how Mulroney and his gang rammed the GST
past Parliament and down our throats

ISBN 0-88910-430-1
ISBN 0-88910-432-8 (counterpack)

1. Goods and services tax — Canada.*
2. Canada. Parliament. Senate.
3. Canada—Politics and government—1984- .*
4. Political ethics.
I. Title.

FC633.G6F7 1991
320.971
C91-095646-4
F1034.2.F75 1991

The man that hath no music in himself,
Nor is not moved with concord of sweet sounds,
Is fit for treasons, stratagems, and spoils,
The motions of his spirit are dull as night,
And his affections dark as Erebus:
Let no such man be trusted.

—William Shakespeare,
The Merchant of Venice, 5.1.84-89

Prologue

"I believe that my privileges were raped and pillaged, and I can tell you that I feel dirty! I feel dirty about the whole thing...."

IN CANADA DEMOCRACY has become an illusion. In reality Canadians are ruled by one person. The Parliament of Canada has become nothing more than a vehicle for the election of a new despotic government in cycles of four or five years.

After each election the leader of the party with the most seats is given the title of Prime Minister, with total power to pick a cabinet from among his or her elected colleagues.[1] The rest of the parliamentarians might as well go home until called upon to initiate the next cycle.

The resulting totalitarian system has evolved in a most remarkable manner: no armed revolution or military coup was required.[2] It has sneaked up on us because Parliament has been doing nothing to stop it from doing so. Indeed, Parliament has been encouraging its own evolution into impotency by quietly lying down and holding still for a slow and painful emasculation process, a process masquerading as the "streamlining" of the parliamentary system. The objective of all streamlining is to increase speed by eliminating resistance. When applied to the parliamentary process it means changing the rules so as to reduce Parliament's resistance and thus increase the government's speed in having its way. And in our system the word government now means the Prime Minister.

With a majority in the House of Commons the Prime Minister wields total power over our new totalitarian system. He picks a cabinet of helpers from among elected followers of his party and can fire any one of them whenever it's convenient. The PM is not accountable to anyone for either the hiring or the firing.

None of these party followers in the House of Commons offers any resistance because every single one of them wants to be in the cabinet and only the Prime Minister can make them so. Those who make a fuss reduce their chances of making it big.

Nor can the Opposition do anything to stop the Prime Minister. It cannot win any votes in the House and its members are only allowed to talk for limited periods. All the talk can be shut off by closure.[3]

In effect, once the leader of the majority party has been sworn in as Prime Minister Parliament is just his or her footstool until the next election. We have reached the stage where Parliament's power is on a par with the Electoral College in the United States, but unlike the Electoral College it is not sent home afterwards. Parliamentarians are ignominiously left to play in their own little playpen until the glorious day when they are again sent out to campaign and become re-elected to pick another Super Boss for another five years.

The slow, agonizing process of parliamentary emasculation has required long conditioning of the patient to guarantee that it held still for the surgery. A few quiet tears of anguish were allowed, but no unseemly hollering and screaming.

In its healthier days, Parliament represented an important element in the distribution or sharing of political power. Most people thought that the otherwise all-powerful government was "responsible" to Parliament. Most of us have heard of the important historical events leading to "responsible government," though most of us were a bit confused about what the word responsible meant in this context.

We thought it meant the government was unable to do what it wanted without the support of Parliament on a daily, ongoing basis. After all, the people didn't elect a prime minister or the cabinet. They were all individually elected only for their own local riding just like scores of others elected at the same time. For instance, in the most recent general election of 1988, 17,639,001 people were eligible to vote in all of Canada, but only 57,275 were eligible to vote for Brian Mulroney in his riding of Charlevoix.[4] So 17,581,726 Canadians weren't even eligible to vote for the potential Prime Minister.

We are no longer as naive as we were when we assumed Parliament could stop a prime minister and his ministerial colleagues from abusing power against the wishes of the people.

Parliamentarians are by nature great talkers. They had to be in order to get elected. And what they are elected to is literally a "talking place," "parler" meaning to discuss or speak. Often they are criticized for not spending enough time in the House of Commons, either talking themselves or listening to others talking.

Our underlying assumption was that someone in government is listening to all this talk. The idea was that the government had to listen to the folks the people had sent there to talk about what the ministers had done or proposed to do. But governments want to *do*, not *talk* about what they want to do. When they do talk it is often either to con the people into letting them go ahead and do whatever it is they want to do or to explain why they had to do what they have already done.

So successive governments have found Parliament, and the need to listen to parliamentarians, a damned nuisance. And governments have been able to persuade the media and the electorate that that is just what Parliament is—a damned nuisance. Especially when parliamentarians went "too far" in partisan resistance to "efficient" government.

No one can show that parliamentary democracy is an efficient form of government. Dictatorships—especially military ones—are infinitely more efficient. The problem is that they are very expensive and inefficient in terms of individual human rights. The system of parliamentary democracy we originally chose for Canada may be slow and inefficient but, as Winston Churchill said, it's still the best anyone has yet devised for the benefit of the governed rather than the governors.

But the system of parliamentary democracy we originally chose for Canada is not the system we have now. It has been transformed by the concentration of power more and more in one person—and so is subject to terrible abuse when, for example, that person has the attitude and style of a bully and, of course, surrounds himself with people of like mind.

Let's take the GST in Parliament's Senate as a case study. Here are some random snippets from the senatorial ruckus of October 4, 1990:

" ... I say to you, Senator Charbonneau, that this act today is a vile act...."

" ... Today, the Speaker of the Senate committed the most grievous sin, a parliamentary sin of unprecedented enormity...."

" ... The Speaker's action was despicable and I see no way in which he can be recognized...."

" ... Shut up, for God's sake! You are a disgrace to this country...."

" ... A tradition of 120 years is gone! You are a disgrace to that Chair!..."

" ... You are a disgrace!..."

" ... You are a bloody disgrace!..."

" ... Don't let this man, who is taking his orders, unfortunately, from the Prime Minister, trample on the rights of the democratic institution...."

... The Hon. the Speaker: "Get back to your seat!"
Some Hon. Senators: "Resign! Sit down! There is no order!"
Senator Perrault: "You have no more authority here!"
An Hon. Senator: "Sit down! You are a disgrace, a goddamned disgrace!..."

" ... I am sorry to say this, but I do not think there are very many senators who have confidence in the Speaker, enough confidence to allow him to carry on, and that is sad. But that is the situation...."

" ... He has his name in this great book about the Speakers of the Senate. All of a sudden he has become a disgrace...."

" ... You are a disgrace to the Canadian parliamentary system, and you should hang your head in shame, sir. The day you step out of that chair I may be prepared to retract my words, but, until then, I want to tell you that I think you are a Brian Mulroney flunky and should be ashamed of yourself, because I am ashamed of you...."

" ... I believe that my privileges were raped and pillaged, and I can tell you that I feel dirty! I feel dirty about this whole thing...."

" ... Senator Murray and the Speaker have hijacked the rules today. They have made Parliament illegitimate. Enmities have been created today which will last a lifetime...."

" ... In ten years, in a hundred years, his actions will be cited as despicable, as a serious attack on our democratic system; in a nutshell, as a coup d'état. I hope that Brian Mulroney too has a sense of the duties of friendship and that, when Senator Charbonneau grasps the full horror of his actions and has the decency to render his resignation...."[5]

How is it possible that people who spent their lives earning a reputation for reasonable speech and behaviour, all experienced parliamentarians never known for unparliamentary outbursts, would have so rudely addressed the Canadian Senate's Speaker, Guy Charbonneau, whom, until that day, they had treated with the greatest respect? What could have caused them to feel so utterly outraged?

What they said and did that night of October 4, 1990, was not planned or orchestrated. It was expressed on the spur of the moment and came from deep inside each individual.

Why didn't the professional observers, the media, try harder to explain why fifty-five senators, all decent, well-behaved people, went so far in rude behaviour and verbal abuse of one of their colleagues who had been appointed their Speaker by Prime Minister Mulroney a few years before?

It turned out to be Parliament's last gasp of resistance to the final act of its emasculation.

Notes

1. If no party has the "most seats"—or a majority—the leader of one of the minority parties tries to form a minority government and the House of Commons decides whether or not to support it and if so for how long. Such minority governments have existed for a total of only twelve years and three months of the 124 years since Confederation.

2. In this case the word "totalitarian" is used in the sense of total concentration of power, rather than its distribution among balancing institutions.

3. Closure cuts off debate by forcing a vote on a specific day at a specific time.

4. Of these 57,275 voters in the Charlevoix riding 33,730 cast ballots for Mulroney.

5. Quotations taken from *Debates of the Senate*, October 4, 1990, pp. 2345 to 2397.

I
The GST — How Do You Like It So Far?

In which Brian has his way with everyone in the House.

WE'VE BEEN PAYING the Goods and Services Tax for close to a year now. During most of 1990, while trying to kick its way through the House of Commons and Senate, that tax bill broke all unpopularity records. To this day its enemies still overwhelmingly outnumber its friends.

If you're one of the enemies, your favourite culprits are probably Brian Mulroney and Michael Wilson. If so, you're letting an equally important wrongdoer escape your wrath: Senate Speaker Guy Charbonneau.

Without him the tax would not now constantly be reminding us, from cash register and invoice, again and again to feed its insatiable appetite for 7 per cent on just about everything.

Even in retrospect it seems reasonable to assume we wouldn't be paying the GST today if the government had been unable to put it in place by January 1, 1991. Even if the government had only had to postpone it rather than drop it and start all over again, it likely would never have gone into effect.

That's why Charbonneau was so vital.

In the law of torts a distinction is made between the *causa causans* (the "causing" cause) and *causa sine qua non* (the cause without which it couldn't have happened anyway). Mulroney and Wilson were the *causae causans* of the GST, but

15

Charbonneau was the *causa sine qua non*. And Charbonneau was needed even after the same Mulroney persuaded Queen Elizabeth to allow him to pack the Senate with Tories to obtain what some still think was an artificial majority.

Here's why.

All national laws must be passed by the House of Commons and the Senate, and then receive royal assent. Parliament consists of the Queen, the Senate and the House of Commons. Even though the Senate is a non-elected body its approval is necessary for any law to take effect. The fact that it is not elected is not acceptable to most Canadians today. Many, including the senators themselves, are demanding that senators be elected as they are in most upper houses in the world. But until such reform comes about, Canadians should, and for the GST legislation *did*, make use of the Senate the way it is currently put together.

Remember the terrible difficulties the Prime Minister and his cronies had to face in order to force their unpopular tax into law? It all came down to the Senate and its rules. This even after the disgraceful use of the Monarchy to ram legislation through Parliament.

Parliamentary rules are a part of the supremacy of the rule of law. The mightiest forces of law and Constitution—the Prime Minister, most provincial premiers, the House of Commons, and most provincial legislatures—were unable to force Meech Lake through because of a few lines in the Manitoba legislature's rule book, and because neither Premier Gary Filmon, the Manitoba Speaker, or anyone else could be persuaded to break that rule to frustrate Elijah Harper.

If Mulroney had been able to persuade Filmon and the Manitoba Speaker to do what Charbonneau did, we'd probably be stuck with Meech Lake as well as the GST.

Senate rules are radically different from the House of Commons rules. Senate rules have maintained, at least on paper, a series of checks and balances over an autocratic government—a system of damage control that the House of Commons gave up some years ago when it accepted rules for closure and allocation of time on speeches.

As we've said, a prime minister with a majority already is in full control of his cabinet and the House of Commons. In addition he has the absolute power to put an early end to any debate even on the most crucial matters and to force opposition members to shut up. Debate by members of Parliament becomes a formality. Here then is a totalitarian government, headed by a prime minister with the total power we've already discussed.

Picture yourself as a member of cabinet when the Prime Minister proposed continuing the pressure to ram through the GST. You've been catching the devil from your constituents, but, as we've noticed, you are appointed by the Prime Minister alone, as were all of your cabinet colleagues. He can, at his own discretion or whim, remove you whenever he wants to without consulting anyone. Out in the House of Commons are some 150 or more of your party colleagues and each one of them would dearly love to replace you in your cabinet seat. The Prime Minister can show you the door and let somebody else in to take your seat, any time he wants.

Now in walks the Prime Minister insisting on his GST no matter what your constituents are telling you. Are you or any of your colleagues likely to give him any serious trouble? Are any of you a "check or balance" against his totality of power?

So it isn't hard to imagine why cabinet wouldn't want to disagree with what the Prime Minister wants. The matter then goes out to the House of Commons. There sit your party colleagues, any one of whom would be glad to replace you in the cabinet, if only the Prime Minister would give him or her the nod. Are they likely to give the Prime Minister any trouble? Are they a check and balance?

What about the Opposition?

All it can do is talk ... for a few hours.

The Opposition leadership can arrange for several MPs to talk for an allocated number of minutes; but only for as long as the Prime Minister or his House Leader decides not to look at his watch and say: "Talk if you like, but at 5:45 on Monday, there will be a vote and my majority will carry it. Meantime we'll humour you by letting you talk."

In other words neither the government supporters in the cabinet or House of Commons nor opposition members can offer anything in the way of real checks or balances.

In the fall of 1990, however, the Senate had neither a limitation on the length of speeches, nor provision to force a vote within a certain time.

Result: even the majority the Queen gave Mulroney for his GST could not have steamrollered a minority that was prepared to go all the way in fighting the tax.

So how did it get passed? We'll see....

II

The Players and the Stage

The importance of being intimate ... with Brian.

FIRST, THE PLAYERS: Guy Charbonneau. Old pal of Mulroney from way back to Iron Ore and Union Nationale days, president of a very successful insurance company in Montreal, and Mulroney fund-raising gold-medallist for many years. Appointed to the Senate in September, 1979, by Joe Clark, and appointed as Speaker of the Senate by Brian Mulroney five years and one month later.

Another pause for another difference between the Senate and the House of Commons.

The Speaker of the House of Commons has always been elected. True, until recently it was a *pro forma* election. By that I mean the Prime Minister picked the Speaker of the House of Commons, but always consulted with opposition leaders, and the house then went through the motions of an election.

But since September 30, 1986, the Speaker of the House of Commons has been genuinely elected by the members, and as a result, of course, has significant powers, really enjoying as he does the confidence of the majority that elected him.

Not so in the Senate.

Ever since Confederation the Speaker of the Senate is directly appointed by the Prime Minister of the day. In fact, the senator arrives and announces to his or her colleagues that he has the honour to inform them that he has been appointed Speaker. Clearly an anomaly, because the Speaker is supposed to *speak* for the members of whatever legislative assembly he presides over and, one would think, should be picked by them, not by an outsider.

The anomaly has some corollaries.

Over the years the senators, having been told who their Speaker is, have, at least metaphorically, replied: "Well, in that case you sit there and call the orders as they come up and we'll ask you if we want you to intervene to call for order or to make any rulings; and when you do make any such rulings (made only when we ask you to) we retain the right to overrule those rulings by a majority vote. If the Prime Minister is going to tell us who our Speaker is rather than our picking him or her, *we're* going to run things here!"

If you have watched House of Commons proceedings on television, you may have noticed another demonstration of this difference in Speakers' roles. You'll have noticed that members of the House of Commons always open their comments by addressing "Mr. Speaker."

But senators ignore the Speaker. They address their colleagues directly, both initially and thereafter. They say, "Honourable Senators," never "Mr. Speaker."

Comparisons therefore between the Speaker of the House of Commons and the Speaker of the Senate are really useless except to underline the differences. For example, the Speaker of the Senate is not the head of the Senate's administration. The Committee of Senators on Internal Economy, Budgets and Administration runs the place. Charbonneau managed to get himself elected for a few years to the chairmanship of this committee early in his tenure.

But the important thing is that the Speaker of the Senate is a mere figurehead. He is there simply to read the prayers, call the orders of the day, preside over votes and otherwise serve the senators in accordance with their rules.

So there we have the *institutional* setting of the GST before the Queen gave Mulroney permission to indulge in an orgy of senatorial appointments.

The *political* setting featured an Opposition Liberal majority with control of all committees, control of votes in the Senate, and able to overrule a speaker.

In the spring of 1990 the Liberals could have defeated the GST. But we didn't have the collective will. If we had had the will then we might very well have killed the GST deader than a dodo. The problem was that Liberal senators were far from united in their wish to do so, until they'd had a chance to hear more from the Canadian people.

At the same time, on the Tory side, the government's objective had to be to get enough Tories to win votes, *plus* a Speaker prepared to assist them to ignore Senate rules and override minority opposition prepared to use those rules to defeat the tax.

That was the scene in the spring of 1990 when the GST drama started to warm up in the Senate.

III

Thermometer Rising

Would the Senate have the guts to kill the bill?

THINGS STARTED TO warm up in the Senate as soon as the GST Bill arrived on the scene. And it's important to remember that at that time the Senate was still, as they say, dominated by Liberals.

Scene One: A meeting of the Senate Liberal caucus, March 1990. What are we going to do with the GST? Lots of discussion but no clear consensus. Many senators vaguely in support of the necessity of a Goods and Services Tax, notably certain Western senators: Bud Olson and Daniel Hays, both from Alberta, and Sidney Buckwold from Saskatchewan. All of them strong on fiscal and financial responsibility. Of those opposed, most of them are not from the financial-interest sector, for example Charles Turner of London, former railway engineer and union man, also many Atlantic senators.

How did the caucus members read the mood of the country? Mixed, just like their own feelings.

A decision was made to refer the bill quickly to a committee for study, possibly at cross-country hearings so as to get a feel for the public mood.

But what committee? Should a special committee be struck? Or how about the Standing Committee on Banking, Trade and Commerce (the normal committee for the GST's subject matter)?

After some discussion the caucus decided on the latter course. Senator Buckwold of Saskatoon recently had been made chairman. He was up for retirement in about a year and a half so he was keen on a kick finish to his long and distinguished political career. Also, at that stage, he was open-minded about the tax.

So when the GST Bill came up in the Senate a rather brief debate on its principle ensued, and, as planned, we voted to send it along to Banking, Trade and Commerce.

Now, the hearings.

Most committee hearings take place in Ottawa. Committee travel requires Senate permission and funding. Conservative supporters obviously would be opposed to taking the Committee on the road. They would argue that the House of Commons committee (where the government had a huge and oppressive majority control) had already dealt fully with the GST. But this frequent government argument comes down to a rubber-stamp or branch-plant role for the Senate, and if the Senate is just a branch plant of the House of Commons, why have it at all?

With the Liberal majority on Banking, Trade and Commerce to vote in favour of the hearings and, if neces-sary, a majority on Internal Economy to vote the necessary funds, our caucus gave the green light to the Committee chairman and the Liberal Committee members to implement the decision to hold cross-country hearings.

As Deputy Leader of the Opposition I was an *ex-officio* member of the Committee, but for most of the hearings I was only involved as a listener to caucus reports from col-leagues.[1] Those reports confirmed media stories about the determination of Tory opposition from Senators Flynn, Simard and others to wreck the Committee hearings as much as possible by rancour, points of order, insults to the chairman, insults to the witnesses, anything to disrupt, discredit and derail the Committee.

But the Committee ploughed on with hearings in Ottawa, Charlottetown, Moncton, St. John's, Halifax, Montreal, Toronto, Winnipeg, Regina, Edmonton, Yellowknife and Vancouver. And finally back to Ottawa.

Word started to drift back that these stormy sessions were playing to packed houses and that the witnesses, although varying widely in composition, did not vary much in opposition and that the doubtful Liberal senators might be starting to change their position about the tax.

This went on for most of the summer of 1990.

On Wednesday, August 8, from Vancouver, I got an unexpected telephone call from Senator Paul Lucier, a Yukon Liberal, who had been a very active participant in the hearings, particularly in the West.

"Look, you better understand that there has been a complete change in the attitude of Liberal senators serving on this Committee," he said. "Those starting out opposed to the tax are even more opposed, but even the Westerners and others who had been mildly in favour of the tax, or at least open-minded, including Olson, Hays, Buckwold and Perrault, are now violently opposed to the tax and are thinking seriously of recommending that the Committee ask the Senate to kill the bill."

Despite government and some editorial rantings about "systematic obstruction," the "Liberal-dominated Senate" had passed more than 95 per cent of Mulroney's legislation without amendment. It had amended only a few bills—and had defeated none.

Very rarely does the Senate defeat legislation, maybe once every forty or fifty years. It slows legislative bills down. It even holds long hearings in order to give the public time to get interested in what is going on. The Senate is the chamber of sober second thought; it's there to try to act as a check and balance, digging in only on those rare occasions when a government with a majority in the House of Commons seems to be going much too far or too fast. As we now know, the opposition in the Commons can't stop the government from doing what it wants to do, because the government can slap time allocation on speeches and force closure to put through any bill whenever it wants. It can't do that in the Senate, at least not according to Senate rules as they then were.

So, yes, killing the GST would be a big deal for the Senate. That phone call was important. Lucier was anything but hysterical. He was an emotional, highly principled guy, but pretty streetwise and tough.

So I didn't waste any time getting in touch with Senator Allan MacEachen, the Leader of the Opposition in the Senate. He decided we'd wait and talk to the Liberal members of the Committee when they got back to Ottawa.

From the beginning and throughout, Senator Jean-Maurice Simard and some of the other Conservatives had been convinced that our plan was to kill the bill and that the hearings were just a sham. This was a plausible theory, but it was wrong. At that point, as I said, we could have done it but we didn't have the will. Our people were not in consensus that the tax should be killed. The tax was perceived to be not without merit, and many Liberal senators, Bud Olson for example, felt that the Senate should rarely, if ever, set itself up against the House of Commons on tax matters. That's why his change of mind, brought about by what the people told him on the road with the Committee, recalled Saint Paul's conversion on the road to Damascus.

Up to that point, as a caucus, we had made no decision about the bill. But Senator Simard, a politically experienced, fierce, life-long Conservative from New Brunswick, was still convinced that we intended to kill the bill, and although he had been wrong in the spring, and wrong for most of the Committee hearings in the summer, he was starting to be right because the sentiment on our side for killing the bill was clearly gaining momentum.

About this time, early August, the media were beginning to show an interest in the possibility that Mulroney would try to pack the Senate.

According to the Constitution the Senate is made up of a maximum of 104 Senators. In August 1990 there were 52 Liberals, 31 Conservatives, 4 Independents, 1 Independent Liberal, 1 Reform Party, and 15 vacancies.

As expected, Mulroney started using his right to fill all the vacancies with new Tory Senators. He did it in batches, but he soon had all vacancies filled. Even then the Liberals still had a majority with their 52, against 46 Conservatives.

To have his way the Prime Minister had to do more than fill all the vacancies. What he did was to dig up an obscure, never-before-used, 123-year-old section of the Constitution:

> If at any Time on the Recommendation of the Governor General the Queen thinks fit to direct that Four or Eight Members be added to the Senate, the Governor General may by Summons to Four or Eight qualified Persons (as the Case may be), representing equally the Four Divisions of Canada, add to the Senate accordingly.

At this point in early August the use of Section 26 seemed remote because the conditions of Senate/Government confrontation and deadlock did not exist, at least not the conditions imposed on the only other occasion when a Prime Minister had actually tried unsuccessfully to use Section 26.[2]

The Committee had promised a report for the fall but had three more days of hearings in Ottawa (on August 29, 30 and 31). They would have to settle down then to draft a report, including a draft of a summary of the background material and evidence. The latter was being worked on in advance because of the early target date for final report to the Senate: September 25.

Through the spring and summer the Tory senators had been accusing the Liberals of delay and urging them to get the Committee hearings over and done with. As we'll see they soon changed that tune when the shoe changed feet.

Notes

1. The Liberals serving on the Committee's cross-country hearings were: Adams, Anderson, Austin, Bonnell, Bosa, Buckwold, Cools, Corbin, De Bané, Fairbairn, Frith, Gigantès, Graham, Guay, Haidasz, Hastings, Hays, Hébert, Kenny, Kirby, Kolber, Leblanc, Lefebvre, Lewis, Lucier, Marsden, Olson, Perrault, Rizzuto, Steuart, Stollery, Thériault.

2. In 1873 Alexander Mackenzie, Canada's first Liberal prime minister, tried to use the section to overcome a Tory Senate majority. Queen Victoria refused to go along with it. Her British advisors apparently told her the right conditions didn't exist because there was no actual obstruction of bills sent to the Senate and no "difference between the two Houses of so serious and permanent a character that the Government could not be carried on without ... (the Queen's) ... intervention" or ... "that the ... (appointments) ... would apply an adequate remedy." These conditions were not present in September, 1990, for Mulroney either; however, Queen Elizabeth didn't refuse; and so far Canadian courts have said she didn't have to.

IV
Back from Patrol and Opening Skirmish

The Senate's civilized atmosphere goes down the drain.

THE COMMITTEE HAD four options: they could pass the GST Bill, delay it, amend it by creating a long list of exemptions to the tax, or they could kill it outright. On August 27 Senator Allan MacEachen and I met, in his office, as planned, with Senators Sidney Buckwold, Bud Olson, Paul Lucier, Earl Hastings, Michael Kirby, Lorne Bonnell and Lorna Marsden—all active on the Committee during its cross-country odyssey.

Senator MacEachen started the meeting by asking what the Committee majority wanted to recommend as the result of its hearings.

Chairman Sid Buckwold reported strong opinion for amendment and mused about delay so opponents could mount support.

Nova Scotia Senator Kirby's polling information confirmed 75 to 80 per cent public opposition to the GST. He felt that massive amendments would be very difficult; they would be highly technical. So it really came down to delay or defeat.

Senator Olson of Alberta was convinced that most Canadians simply didn't want this kind of tax. The Committee had been deluged by evidence of collection difficulties and accounting and bookkeeping problems in exchange for nothing of benefit to the vendor upon whom the obligations would fall. He felt the tax had simply not been thought through and agreed that 75 to 80 per cent of the people seemed to be against the legislation, including businessmen who simply couldn't afford the additional staff.

Senator Buckwold, the Committee chairman, reminded us that the provincial premiers were also strongly opposed to it.

There was still some feeling about the need for an alternative proposal.

We also had to consider the question of linkage to free trade and the feelings of Senators Leo Kolber, George Van Roggen and some others who had questioned the Liberal Party's wobbly stand on the Free Trade Agreement in 1988, because every vote was going to count if we were to take the serious action being contemplated.

Public interest through most of September was focused by the media on installment Tory appointments to the vacancies and the fact that, even if they were all filled, the GST could not become law over Liberal opposition unless the Prime Minister was permitted to stack the Senate by using Section 26 of the Constitution.

All fifteen vacancies were filled, but the appointees could not take their seats until the Senate resumed on September 25. And even then, as noted, the Liberal Opposition would still have a numerical majority. So media and other attention continued to be focused on the use of Section 26 to stack the Senate with enough Tory senators to force the tax through.

The Committee report target was Tuesday, September 25. The previous week Senator MacEachen and I met to work out a strategy with Senator Buckwold and other Committee members.

The plan was to prepare the main body of the report as a summary of the evidence and research data, and to word it so it could form the basis for any one of the four options—pass, delay, amend or defeat.

By this time we could hear the clock ticking towards a showdown Committee vote.

The draft report was to be ready when the Committee met at 1:30 p.m. on Monday, September 24, the day before the Senate resumed.

It was agreed that the "body" of the report, to be written by the staff, would not be controversial since it was simply a summary of the research and evidence. This would leave it up to the Committee itself to make the fundamental decision —pass, delay, amend or defeat.

Obviously the Conservative members, a minority, would opt for passage without amendment. By that time the Liberals had decided to opt for a recommendation that the bill "not be proceeded with"—parliamentary jargon for kill the bill.

On Monday, September 24, the Liberal Committee members had a luncheon meeting to develop tactics. We already had decided with Senator MacEachen that we wanted the Committee to decide that afternoon to have the report ready for presentation to the Senate when it resumed sitting on Tuesday, hoping to win the race against any packing of the Senate with Tories.

I pointed out that to meet that objective we would have to be very tough minded and bring on a vote of the Committee that afternoon. But there seemed no reason to prolong discussion: the options available to the Committee were plain. We realized it wouldn't take the Tories long to figure out that we intended to flex whatever muscle we still had to kill the bill in the same way as they would no doubt want to flex what muscle they had to ram it through.

The meeting was in room 250 in the East Block with lots of reporters and TV cameras before the meeting began. The meeting itself would be in private as is usually the case when preparing a report.

At 1:30 sharp the Tories had a full turnout and so did we. A quick count showed we had the majority to achieve our objectives. As soon as Chairman Buckwold called the meeting to order it became apparent that the government supporters were geared up for a crucial battle.

One of the first questions they raised was whether this meeting, though *in camera*, required a transcript to be taken by Senate reporters. Such reporters, of course, attend and take records of Senate committee meetings in the normal course, but it is not usually done for *in camera* hearings.

As anticipated, there was also a good deal of fuss about insufficient time to read the summary of the evidence taken during the summer, but after a number of understandable objections about the lack of such time it soon became apparent to us that the Tories meant to filibuster the Committee meeting to prevent the majority from deciding to recommend killing the bill.[1] It was equally apparent to them that that was precisely what we meant to do, and meant to do that very day.

Such a fierce locking of horns is extraordinary in Senate committees, but so was everything that led up to the passing of the GST. And the unusual chemistry that started in that committee room remained for all the fall months right up to a few days before Christmas. In fact the old "gentlemen's club" atmosphere still has not returned.

The meeting was long and rowdy.

The Tories, led by Senator William Doody, made long, impassioned speeches about the impossibility of deciding how to vote without time to read the summary of the evidence. Our side responded with equal passion that the report simply summarized evidence already familiar to members of the Committee and that the Committee was right then in a position to choose among the options—pass, delay, amend or reject.

Things became even more explosive when I suggested we should make a decision by seven o'clock that evening. After much weeping, wailing and gnashing of teeth on all sides, and continued outraged protests from the Tories, the Committee members came to a vote (all Liberals for, all Conservatives against), carrying the motion that the bill "not be proceeded with"—effectively killing the GST if the Senate adopted the report.

The *next* day, before the Senate sitting scheduled for two o'clock, we met in Liberal caucus, with our new leader, Jean Chrétien, in attendance. He agreed with our caucus that we should push for Senate adoption of the Committee's report killing the bill.

At the Committee the *previous* day, several of the "new" vacancy-filling senators appeared, although they had not been sworn in, because the Senate had not met since their appointment.

When the Senate resumed at two o'clock on Tuesday, after Tory complaints about the Committee's activity the preceding day had been raised by several Conservative senators with the obvious intention of filibustering the Committee's report, thirteen new senators were sworn in. Two more had been appointed but did not show up.

As a result of these fifteen appointments party standing was: Conservatives 46, Liberals 52, Independent 4, Reform 1, Independent Liberal 1, for a total of 104.

Senator Lowell Murray, the government leader in the Senate, assured the Senate that "the other two will not be long delayed," and he then went on to express his "entire satisfaction with the number of reinforcements who have arrived today." He proceeded at length to praise the thirteen who had been sworn in that day. These extensive eulogies turned out to be part of a filibuster to block presentation of the Committee's "killer" report.

There then followed long filibustering questions of privilege from Tory Senators Gerald Ottenheimer, Jean-Marie Poitras, Brenda Robertson, Jean-Maurice Simard, Staff Barootes, William Doody and others about the proceedings in the Committee meeting the previous day.

The very long series of speeches that followed argued about whether proceedings in the Committee were a matter for the Committee or for the Senate. The Speaker was finally asked for an opinion and he asked for time to consider.

That brought the order paper to the heading of committee reports, where the killer report understandably was the featured item.[2] Senator Ottenheimer then wanted to continue the filibuster to prevent Senator Buckwold from presenting the Committee's report. The floor should have belonged to the chairman of the Committee, but Ottenheimer insisted the Speaker had recognized him. I think Senator Charbonneau already was assisting the government by delaying the committee reports—including Senator Buckwold's presentation of the report killing the GST Bill.

The killer report continued to be filibustered by the government side until the next day, Wednesday (September 26), giving the Conservatives time to set up the royal stacking.

On Wednesday, the Speaker ruled, in effect, that committee procedures were a matter for the Committee and that it was not feasible to turn back the clock and prevent the presentation of the Committee report on allegations of procedural breaches.

34

It then seemed we were on our way to presentation of the killer report to the Senate that day, even if we couldn't deal with it until the following day under Senate rules.

But no. The Tory filibuster was not yet exhausted.

When the Committee report was again called Senator Buckwold only got to present it and was unable to ask that it be dealt with in accordance with the rules the following day, because Senator Murray jumped to his feet with another point of order.

He objected that the Committee ought to have gone through the bill clause by clause. This point of order had been disposed of by the Speaker's ruling a few moments earlier, but, of course, that is never a problem in a filibuster, since the object of the filibuster is simply to keep talking for delay purposes, as the Liberals eventually did for their purposes.

The Speaker's opinion given later on Senator Murray's point was indeed that it was simply a repetition of the earlier point. Speaker Charbonneau then added that "there is an obligation on the part of all Honourable Senators whether they be in the Senate or in the Committees of the Senate, that notwithstanding their Party affiliations and the seriousness of the great questions that are before them, they obey the Rules, Customs and Traditions of the Senate at all times."

If only he himself would later have taken his own sermon to heart.

Notes

1. The filibuster is a weapon minorities in legislatures sometimes use, or try to use, when threatened by what they feel is abusive use of majority power. It can't be used frequently because majority rule is legitimately supported by most people who therefore won't give public support to a

filibuster unless convinced that majority rule is being abused. A fili-buster's substance is always to gain time—short, medium or long—by a minority against a majority. The Tories, at that time in the minority, were to use it that day, and later, to the hilt to prevent the Liberals from defeating the GST. But very soon they would be blaming the Liberals for using it against them, when they, the Tories, had the majority and then wanted to force the tax through.

2. The "Order Paper" establishes the order in which business is done each day in the Senate. Rule 19, effective then and throughout the GST battle, sets the order of business as follows:

> 19. At each daily sitting of the Senate, the Speaker shall call for, in the following order: (a) presentation of petitions; (b) reading of petitions; (c) reports of committees; (d) notices of inquiries; (e) notices of motions; (f) question period; (g) orders of the day; (h) inquiries; (i) motions.

Item (g)—"orders of the day"—is where legislation is set out and where, therefore, Bill C-62, the GST Bill, would be listed. So the enforcement of this rule about order of business and "orders of the day" in it became a crucial factor in delaying the GST in the Senate.

V

No Longer Dominated by Liberals

Should we import some linebackers from the Buffalo Bills?

T HE NEW NUMBERS meant that we Liberals had to be very careful to be sure there would only be a vote when we could guarantee a turnout of enough Liberals to win it.

The crucial vote, of course, was the vote to adopt the Banking, Trade and Commerce Committee report. That would kill the GST for the session. If the government were still determined to go ahead with the tax it would have to start all over again in the House of Commons, after a new Speech from the Throne.

At a Wednesday morning strategy meeting we went over the various possibilities for delay—by filibuster tactics, long question periods, petitions, adjourning the Senate, adjourning debate and a lesser-known esoteric technique about the presence of "strangers in the House," a motion that must be put without debate.

We had no idea then how soon we would need to use this obscure technique, but we did have an uneasy feeling that the additional eight royal stackers were being lined up for a swearing-in ceremony outside the Senate. We had been dismayed to find out that this was a valid procedure, for the chamber is the usual place for swearing-in ceremonies.

The filibuster by the government supporters on points of order continued, and that and other matters kept the Senate busy until it adjourned at 8:30 that night, Wednesday, September 26.

The following afternoon at two o'clock the Tory filibuster was resumed right after prayers. This time the clever devils made a whole series of lavish tributes to Conservative Senator Martha Bielish who had decided to resign early in order to make room for a replacement.[1] The normal tributes were offered, but then they went on and on and on. It became clear the Tories were exploiting Senator Bielish's retirement to kill time.

Senator Joyce Fairbairn came into the Senate chamber (she sits right behind me) and said that there was something fishy going on in the Speaker's office with the clerk involved in some ceremony. It didn't require special brilliance to realize this had to do with the royal stacking. In fact the royal stackers had been sneaked, à la Stalag 17, from the East Block through an underground tunnel to the Centre Block near a stairway up to the Speaker's main floor office.

As the tributes to Senator Bielish became more beatification than tribute, we became sure something tricky was going on so I used the "strangers" motion to force an adjournment of the Senate.

Most legislatures and other deliberative bodies reserve the right to exclude non-members ("strangers") on certain occasions, and the Senate rule book has a provision to do so. It is hardly ever used except for tactical purposes. Its value is that any senator can take notice of the presence of such "strangers" and the Speaker or committee chairman immediately has to put the question "that strangers be ordered to withdraw" *without permitting any debate or amendment.*

The Speaker and the clerk's officers at their table were surprised by the motion, but I pointed out to them that the rule was very clear that the motion had to be put on the spot without debate. Our purpose was to get time to plan, because once the motion was put, a standing vote would be forced and the bells would ring and the vote could not be taken until both whips were ready to enter, as the Senate rule book provides.[2]

The experts sitting at the clerk's table in the Senate advised the Speaker that he had no choice but to put the motion, and he did so.

The standing vote was forced and the Speaker then made the usual order to "call in the senators." The bells began to ring and the senators dispersed waiting for their whips to call them back for the vote.

The Senate rule book provides that a vote cannot be held until the whips enter the Senate, thus signifying that their respective sides are ready for the vote. As far as I know the rules of all legislatures around the world provide for the same procedure, or something very like it, because the holding of a vote before both sides are ready wouldn't make any sense, or at least could not be said to capture the sense of the legislature, the whole purpose of the vote.

Later that day Senators MacEachen, Jacques Hébert and I held a press conference at the Press Building theatre to explain our position and I stopped on my way home for a bite of dinner. I had not been there long when I received a call from Len Kuchar, Senator MacEachen's special assistant, suggesting that I call Senator MacEachen because Speaker Charbonneau had ordered the bells to be silenced.

This was a stunner. Silencing of the bells in the Senate was quite unheard of. That Senator Charbonneau had admitted to me that he had decided on his own to do so was astonishing.

Senator Charbonneau had sent a letter explaining why he had made this decision, and while the idea of silencing the bells for the weekend to start them up again when the whips were ready was not in itself a scandalous idea, what we were outraged about was that Senator Charbonneau had decided to do so completely on his own.

I was told I could reach Senator Charbonneau at a restaurant in Ottawa. I called him there and we had a heated exchange about where he found authority unilaterally to shut off the bells. I ended by saying I would be in his office the following morning to continue the protest about his unprecedented decision to shut off the bells without authorization by the Senate and even without any consultation.

I spoke to Charbonneau the next morning, Friday September 27, again by telephone, before leaving home for my Senate office. I told him that I would be in his office shortly. He said he did not want to discuss it without both sides present. That was fine with me. I would be there and I hoped he would arrange for Senator Murray, leader of the government, or his representative, also to be there.

I then went to Senator MacEachen's office in the Senate. We called Senator Charbonneau and were told that he was not available, that he was on his way to Montreal. He had said nothing the night before or that morning about having to be in Montreal that day, and left no explanation as to why he had taken off.

Senator MacEachen and I then discussed the question of the bells with Senator Gil Molgat, the elected Deputy Speaker and chairman of the Rules Committee. We asked him if he had ever heard of such a thing as Senator Charbonneau's unilateral action in shutting off the bells. He hadn't.

The three of us then went to the office of the clerk, Mr. Gordon Barnhart, taking with us Senator Charbonneau's letter. We asked the clerk if he knew of any basis for such shutting off of the bells and confirmed with him that votes and bells for votes were governed by the rule book, which stipulates that the bells were stopped and votes taken only when both whips signified that they were ready. We wanted no room whatever for doubt on the question or the clerk's position on it. The three of us left with the clerk unequivocally assuring us that there was no rule, provision, tradition or other justification for the holding of a vote *until the whips had entered signifying their readiness for the vote.*

Before we left for the weekend Senators MacEachen, Molgat and I discussed our surprise at Senator Charbonneau's audacity in doing what he did. At the time, I never considered the possibility that Senator Charbonneau might be deliberately subverting the rules of the Senate, a conclusion I came to only much later. My explanation was that it was just stupid—I had never believed that Speaker Charbonneau had any sense for parliamentary traditions or procedures. I think Senator Molgat tended to agree, but the ever-canny Senator MacEachen was much more suspicious. We decided to leave it at that because, after all, Senator Charbonneau at some point was going to have to come back from Montreal to face the rule-book music that we were now sure prevented his dancing to his own tune.

On Monday, October 1, Senator MacEachen, Len Kuchar and I continued discussions about the qualifications of the royally stacked senators and how we could prevent them taking their seats and voting. Naturally a good deal of the discussion centred on their qualifications under Section 26 and the right of the Prime Minister and the Queen to install them in the Senate. That discussion was continued the following day and later at a meeting with Senators Kirby, Molgat, John Stewart and J. S. Grafstein regarding a court challenge. Senator Grafstein advised that Edgar Sexton, a very prominent lawyer in Toronto, was interested in the constitutional question, particularly as it related to the fact that New Brunswick would then have more representatives in the Senate than in the House of Commons—something prohibited by the Constitution.

We then went to the Senate Liberal caucus, where we reported on our thoughts about Senator Charbonneau's decision and agreed that we would go in for a vote on my "strangers" motion at two o'clock, but would continue to protest the seating of the "British" senators.

About two o'clock that day the whips entered for the vote but before the vote could be taken Senator Molgat rose on a question of privilege, namely that since the matter of the senators appointed under Section 26 was before the courts, it would be improper for the eight senators to participate in a vote, and at that point they had yet to be officially seated anyway.

Debate on this question continued with long interventions on both sides until the mandatory six o'clock dinner break arrived.

At this point we were ready with more speakers and there was a clear possibility of an all-night session. Senate rules permit round-the-clock sittings, except for a dinner break between six and eight.

So along with my Conservative counterpart—Senator Doody, the deputy government leader and house leader—I worked out an agreement that we would adjourn until two o'clock the next day with the proceedings frozen so everyone's position would remain exactly the same. This was approved by our colleagues. When we resumed at eight o'clock this agreement was put on the record and it was clearly stated that "everyone's position, including the Speaker's, remain exactly the same."

To make it even clearer Senator Douglas Everett asked if "the point of privilege will still be an issue tomorrow."

"Yes, nothing is changed," I answered. No one objected or expressed any lack of understanding about what Senator Doody and I had clearly put on the record. I underline this here because it turned out to be the setting for the next procedural coup by Senator Charbonneau.

When we started the Wednesday (October 3) sitting Senator Charbonneau rose and wanted to begin proceedings by seating the eight new senators.

I immediately objected to the Speaker being on his feet at all because the agreement on the previous day was that we were to be exactly in the position we were at the close of that day, namely in the midst of debate on Senator Molgat's question of privilege. The Speaker had certainly not been on his feet when we adjourned with proceedings frozen "by agreement." When we had adjourned, he was *sitting* (where he should continue to sit), so we could begin with the position exactly as it had been.

But Senator Charbonneau, in spite of the rules, in spite of the agreement, pushed on, stating that he had "the honour" to inform the Senate that he had received a document from the clerk of the Senate showing that the royal eight had "taken and subscribed their oath of allegiance to Her Majesty Queen Elizabeth II" and "had made and subscribed the declaration of property," and so on. He stated that their writs of summons would be printed in the Senate minutes.

As we had guessed, the usual procedure of swearing in the new senators in the chamber had been subverted: they had been sworn in secretly. But even that would not have had them seated in the Senate if the Speaker had not further helped the government get its majority by brazenly ignoring Senate traditions and a specific, Senate-recorded agreement.

Here are the names of those Speaker Charbonneau so "regionally qualified": John Michael Forrestall, Maritimes; James W. Ross, Maritimes; Normand Grimard, Quebec; Thérèse Lavoie-Roux, Quebec; Wilbert Joseph Keon, Ontario; Michael Arthur Meighen, Ontario; Eric Arthur Berntson, Western; Janis Johnson, Western.[3]

He then improperly shoved his way into the proceedings to make a ruling on the question of privilege. According to our agreement, we were supposed to have resumed in exactly the same position we had been in on the previous evening.

We objected, pointing out that the question of privilege debate had not been completed and that Senator MacEachen wished to speak on that point of privilege immediately.

Another uproar ensued, this time over the Speaker's right to step in without invitation from the Senate or authority from the rules.

The official debates reports had been running behind, so during a good deal of this discussion we had no written record of the agreement that we should be in exactly the same position that day. We finally found a transcript; it verified our position, but the Speaker insisted on reserving on the point of order we had raised. The Senate proceeded to tributes to retiring Senator Joe Guay. The Senate then adjourned to the following day.

Wednesday had been a clear success for the government, helped by the improper actions of the Speaker. The Senate record would show that the "gang of eight" were "on the books." The government's systematic obstruction of the report of the Banking, Trade and Commerce Committee killing the GST had, with active partisan help from the Speaker, prevailed for the period of September 26 to October 3, so as to establish for the Prime Minister what we considered an artificial working majority in the Senate.

Mind you, the qualifications of these new Senators were still very much in doubt. But there they were, and short of importing some linebackers from the Buffalo Bills, we had no way of stopping them from taking their seats as long as Speaker Charbonneau broke the rules to let them do so.

Still, when the Senate began its sitting on Thursday—the now-infamous October 4—I still had no idea of what we were really up against, and how far the government was prepared to go.

Senator MacEachen had a long-standing and important engagement in Germany. We discussed whether he should cancel it but since he and I, with others, had planned the tactics for continuing our delay of the GST bill, there was no reason they couldn't be used while he was away for those two or three days; including the stranger's motion, adjournment of the Senate and other possibilities assuming, as we did, that Speaker Charbonneau would now enforce the rules.

At two o'clock on October 4 the Tory Senate seats were full with the fifteen senators appointed to fill vacancies plus the "British" eight. That meant the Speaker could now proceed to do the government's will, knowing that Tory senators could win a vote as long as the Independents didn't support the Opposition. They could also defeat appeals of any of the Speaker's rulings—providing, of course, that the "gang of eight" were allowed to vote. And at this point I certainly wasn't counting on Speaker Charbonneau to disqualify them.

It also meant that Speaker Charbonneau could safely allow the report of the Committee killing the GST to come forward, knowing it would be defeated by the weight added by the new Senators plus the "British" Senators and any Independents who either supported the government or didn't support us.

He was safe too in ruling against the Tories, as he did, that the questions of privilege raised by the Tories during their filibuster to stop presentation of the report were not proper questions of privilege. The authorities were clear; indeed they had been just as clear throughout the Tory filibuster, but if the Speaker had so ruled *at that time* then the Committee report could have been adopted and the GST would have been killed.

He then dealt with the qualifications of the senators. And again he was quite safe in following, not Senate Rule 33 on questions of privilege but the House of Commons procedure. He was perfectly safe now because if the Liberals appealed, the Tories would uphold his ruling.

I argued that there were serious consequences if Charbonneau allowed the stackers to vote. Questions raised in the country about the status of these additional senators were not being settled, as they ought to be, by the Senate itself, and that the senators whose qualifications were challenged could hardly expect to vote on the question in which they had such a direct interest, namely their qualification—being defendant, judge and jury in their own cause.

So I made a motion to adjourn the Senate because I believed that we could not properly do business until these questions had been cleared up; that every senator's privileges were involved because so long as the challenged "gang of eight" were allowed to vote no senator could know whether votes taken were legitimate.

Although I didn't recognize the significance of it at the time, when I moved the adjournment of the Senate, Senator Murray quickly sprung to his feet and said: "When Your Honour calls for the division on this matter my colleagues and I will be standing and calling for a recorded vote." Well, of course, there would be a recorded vote, but I didn't realize then the kind of recorded "vote" he had in mind.

Senators left the chamber as the bells began to ring to "call in the senators" for a vote.

According to the Senate rule book, as explained, that vote could not be taken until the two whips agreed that they were ready and had entered the chamber for the holding of the vote. It's all covered in Part 4 of the rule book and an appendix that lays out the procedure in detail.[4]

In that context, and believing that the Senate rules would apply, we immediately went to caucus. It was only shortly after two o'clock, because the above proceedings had taken only a few moments. We agreed at that caucus that we would not let the bells ring for the weekend but probably would let them ring overnight, thus having an opportunity to talk to Senator MacEachen to bring him up to date and get his advice.

Senator MacEachen was the Leader of the Opposition, both in title and very much in fact, throughout the GST battle as he had been since his appointment in 1984. He was adept at developing strategy and directing tactics. He consulted widely and regularly beforehand but there was never any doubt who was boss and who the caucus wanted to make the final decision.

But we had not anticipated the unbelievable coup the Speaker took during Senator MacEachen's short absence from the country.

So, if you blame anyone for the desk-banging, shouting and other noise-making, blame me because I was making the decisions Senator MacEachen would normally have taken had he not been rushing back from Europe.

Notes

1. Daily sittings of the Senate begin with prayers. As soon as the Speaker arrives the doors are closed and he reads a brief prayer in French and English. The prayer used to be much longer and included lengthy references to the Queen and other less-than-populist institutions. There wasn't a word about the people of Canada. The new very much shorter prayer does refer to the people of Canada and not much else. The routine prayer later turned out to be surprisingly important procedurally in the passage of the GST.

2. A party whip is a senator acting as a sort of sergeant major who has the responsibility (among many others) to get their side's supporters "on parade" for a vote in the legislative chamber (here, the Senate) or in committees.

3. Senators are normally appointed for their province but Section 26, the stacking section, provides for appointment by region—the Maritimes, Quebec, Ontario and the West are the four "regions."

4. Voting in the Senate is described in Rules 49 and 50:

49. (1) When a question is put to a vote, the Speaker shall ask for the "yeas" and the "nays" and shall thereupon decide whether the question has carried.

(2) In the absence of a request for a standing vote, the decision of the Speaker is final.

(3) Upon the request of two senators before the Senate takes up other business, the Speaker shall call for a standing vote, at which time the "yeas" shall first rise in their places, then the "nays," then the abstentions.

(4) A senator is not entitled to vote on any question in which the senator has a pecuniary interest not available to the general public. The vote of any senator so interested shall be disallowed.

(5) Questions arising in the Senate shall be decided by a majority of voices. The Speaker shall in all cases have a vote. When the voices are equal the decision shall be deemed to be in the negative.

50. (1) A senator shall not vote on any question unless the senator is within the Bar of the Senate when the question is put.

(2) Without leave of the Senate a senator shall not speak to a question after the order has been given to call in the members to vote thereon.

(3) With leave of the Senate, the vote of a senator may, for special reasons assigned by the senator, be withdrawn or changed by the senator immediately after the announcement of the division.

At the conclusion of a debate, the Speaker puts the question. If there is uncertainty of agreement, the Speaker asks for the "yeas" and the "nays" and then expresses his opinion as to the result. If two or more senators express their disagreement by rising, the Speaker calls for a standing vote. The division bells are rung, and when the Whips have entered the Chamber and have indicated to the Speaker that they are ready to proceed to the vote, the Speaker should say: "Let the doors of the Chamber be locked." The doors will then be locked by the pages and the Speaker will call for the vote. The Speaker puts the question again. All senators in favour of the motion rise, and the Clerk of the Senate records their names on the division sheet. All senators opposed to the motion rise, and the Clerk records their names on the division sheet. All senators who wish to abstain then rise, and the Clerk records their names on the division sheet. The Clerk announces the official result of the division, giving the number of "yeas," the number of "nays" and the "abstentions." The Speaker then declares the motion carried or lost.

VI
Lock Them Out!

How they hijacked the Senate while I was on the phone to Germany.

ABOUT 4:45 P.M. on October 4, I went to Senator Allan MacEachen's office to telephone him in Germany. I was in the process of explaining to him what had happened when Senator William Petten, our whip, and Senator Joyce Fairbairn came in to say that the Tories seemed to be making plans to proceed with the vote.

At that very moment I received a hand-delivered letter from the Speaker. It had been sent to the Leaders of the Government and Opposition and to the Independent senators, *and only to them*—not to the other senators. It stated that a vote was going to be taken at 5:30 because "of the failure of the mechanisms established by the political parties within the Senate to assemble Senators for a division bell within a reasonable time"—whatever that meant.

I asked our whip, Senator Petten, to go to the Senate entrance and make it clear that we were not ready for a vote. I was reading the Speaker's letter over the phone to Senator MacEachen in Germany, and dictating an answer, when the loudspeaker connecting senators' offices to the Senate came alive with noises indicating the Speaker really planned to have a vote.

With Senator MacEachen on the telephone in Germany and Senator Fairbairn and others telling me about the Tory

51

plans, and at the same time trying to dictate an answer to the letter of Senator Charbonneau, I glanced at the clock. It was showing very close to 5:20 p.m. By now I had my letter completed. It read:

Senator Charbonneau,
I was handed your letter of October 4th, at 5:00 p.m. about the presently ringing division bells, and of your decision to stop the bell and proceed to put the question before the Senate at 5:30 p.m. today.

You have no authority to do so and will be in a direct breach of the procedures established by the Senate as set out on page 70 of the Senate Rule Book. "When the division bells are rung and the whips have entered the Chamber and have indicated to the Speaker that they are ready to proceed to the vote" ... the vote is taken.

I tell you now that our Whip is not ready to enter the Chamber and indicate his readiness to proceed to the vote.

I urge you to reconsider your decision because the consequences of such a blatantly illegal attempt to exercise powers which you do not have are very serious.

I was going to take that letter to Senator Charbonneau when suddenly the loudspeaker came alive again. The sound that came out of the speaker was Senator Charbonneau's voice ordering "Let the doors to the Chamber be locked."

I looked at the clock; it was not later than 5:25. I had to tell Senator MacEachen that the Speaker had locked the doors, although Senator Petten had told his opposite number, Senator Orville Phillips, the Tory whip, that he was not yet ready to go in, and that therefore no vote could be taken, because the procedures set out on page 70 of the rule book were not being followed.

So there we were, Senator MacEachen on the phone in Germany, I in his office discussing what the Speaker's reaction to my letter might be, when suddenly I had to tell Senator MacEachen that our discussion was apparently pointless because I could hear on the loudspeaker the vote being taken behind the locked doors in our absence.

Surely even a Stalin or Hitler would have at least pretended to allow some opposition presence.

Here are the names of the fifty-four "parliamentarians" who voted in the absence of the locked-out opposition, and, of course, not one of them uttering a single word of protest about the outrageous thing they were doing: Atkins, Balfour, Barootes, Beaudoin, Beaulieu, Belisle, Berntson, Bolduc, Buchanan, Carney, Castonguay, Chaput-Rolland, Cochrane, Cogger, Comeau, David, DeWare, Di Nino, Doody, Doyle, Everett (Independent), Eyton, Forrestall, Grimard, Hatfield, Johnson, Kelleher, Kelly, Keon, Kinsella, Lavoie-Roux, Lynch-Staunton, Finlay MacDonald, MacQuarrie, Marshall, Meighen, Molson (Independent), Muir, Murray, Nurgitz, Oliver, Ottenheimer, Phillips, Poitras, Robertson, Roblin, Ross, Rossiter, Simard, Spivak, Sylvain, Teed, Tremblay, Twinn.

Another pause.

Let me ask, dear reader, how you would have reacted in our place?

How would the Tories have reacted in our place?

Let us suppose, for example, we could have persuaded Senator Molgat, the Deputy Speaker and a Liberal, to call a vote on the GST when the government whip wasn't ready and had said so. What would they have said if we had gone ahead and held the vote in their absence, thus killing the GST?

What would their reaction have been and their whip's reaction—and Mulroney's reaction, and Wilson's reaction, André's reaction? What would they have said?

"My goodness. Tsk tsk. Those Liberals should not have killed our GST with an illegal vote, but we will just have to register our objection quietly and swallow the loss of our GST. We must behave like good ladies and gentlemen and let the Grits kill our GST because if we lose our tempers or make any fuss, everyone will criticize us because of the fuss rather than them for their parliamentary crime? So there goes our GST. Too bad"?

Is that what they would have said?

Not a chance.

Of course they wouldn't have tolerated such an outrage.

Neither would you.

Neither did we.

We may have gone further, or perhaps not as far, as you would have gone. Canadians are by nature opposed to confrontation and violent reaction. Perhaps you would not have invited reporters and TV cameras into the chamber to illustrate the kind of anarchy that can follow what we believe was, plain and simple, a dictatorial breach of the rules and the abandonment of the rule of law. Perhaps you would not have shouted, pounded your desks, made any noise you could and even got our your kazoos and tooted them as loud as you could, the only means left to prevent the government from getting the floor to push on with illegal ramming through its GST.

As you probably know, those are some of the things we did during those long endless hours, and accordingly attracted media and other criticism for our behaviour, rather than criticism of the government Speaker's outrage that provoked it.

At that stage noise and shenanigans were the only means we had to prevent the Speaker and government senators from hijacking of the Senate to present a motion that would have been the first step to the passing of the GST. The Speaker and Tory leadership had shown they would simply ride right over any civilized and procedurally correct moves we made. Citing the law to hooligans is a waste of time, but a short dose of anarchy might get their attention. What we did was more than a show of indignation. It was a desperate last resort to convince the government and its supporters in the Senate that their refusal to obey parliamentary law would not get them their way.

But that was all later. First we had to get back into the Senate.

Of course, we could have simply stayed out and sulked.

That would have been perfect from Mulroney, Murray and Charbonneau's point of view. They could then have laughed their way to immediate passage of their GST and anything else they wanted.

What we had to do was to make trouble, lots of trouble, all we could to stop them. But this was something we couldn't do from outside the Senate chamber. Any battles outside the chamber had to be waged mostly by the people and the media.

VII
The Long, Hot, Noisy Nights

Cancel the turkey, dear.

A S SOON AS the doors were opened after the "vote," I went into the Senate chamber. It was probably no later than 5:40 p.m., because the vote had been taken right after the doors had been locked at 5:25.

Already the orders of the day were being called, in what looked like an attempt to try to race ahead to the order dealing with the GST in the hope of ramming it through before the opposition could say a word.

In retrospect, I am convinced that this was all part of the "plan" that Michael Wilson, then Minister of Finance, had stated was in place to get his GST bill through the Senate that week.

Earlier in the week Wilson had told Mike Duffy, the television host and columnist, that the government had a "plan" to get the bill through by the end of the week, and, as he put it, "That's not just bravado, Mike!"

Anyway, we were more concerned, at that moment, about the outrage that had been committed on the Senate, and really on the whole parliamentary system, by the Speaker helping the government by holding a vote in the absence of the Opposition and in direct contravention of Senate rules.

So I stood up and recounted, as above, the events following receipt of the Speaker's letter at five o'clock.

The rest of the day was understandably taken up with expressions of incredulous outrage at the breach of the privilege of every senator, if not of every parliamentarian, by this insane holding of a "vote" with only one side present.

Some thirty-five Liberal senators participated in indicting the Speaker and those who voted. No Tory senator offered any defence.

By four o'clock the next morning, after listening to eight hours of debate on the question of privilege, during which we said we would try our best to prevent any business being done as long as Senator Charbonneau was in the chair, everyone was still pumped up; and no end was in sight.

Senator Charbonneau had asked various Tory senators to replace him in the chair. Senator Nathan Nurgitz accepted and was in the chair in the early-morning hours, trying to call orders of the day to get to the GST Bill.

Finally I went to Senator Nurgitz in the chair and said I was prepared to talk to the government leadership about a solution, providing I was satisfied he would leave the chair, that no one else would take the chair, and that nothing would take place in the Senate while we were talking. He agreed.

I met with Senators Doody and Murray. We agreed to suspend everything until after the Thanksgiving weekend for a cooling-off period. We would allow the Senate to get to the killer report the following Tuesday. That is we agreed to allow it to be *called*, nothing beyond that point.

I had gathered our group together in Senator Molgat's office, and explained what I had agreed to recommend, namely that we would postpone orders of the day numbers 1, 2, 3 and 4 dealing with legislation other than the GST, and would allow the Committee's report on the GST to be called.

It was then about 5:40 in the morning. We had all been in the Senate for the whole of the previous day and night, but before adjourning Senator Doody and I put on the record what we had agreed to, namely that we would allow debate to start on the report on the GST, that Senator Buckwold would simply move the adoption of the report, say a word or two about it, and then we would adjourn the debate. Again, everyone's position was to remain the same.

We would be starting a fresh sitting on October 9. This was very important, because it meant that we would be at the top of the order paper, and the item at the top of the order paper was *not* the GST. It was under "orders of the day," well down the line after petitions, notices, question period, and so on.

The postponement at 5:40 a.m. on October 5 was simply to get the Committee report debate on the order paper. There was no agreement as to what we would do with orders 1, 2, 3 and 4, which dealt with other legislation. This meant that we had not agreed to do anything except to have the GST Committee report on the order paper *after* the other items relating to legislation under "orders of the day," itself well down the line on the order paper.

So that was how things looked on the morning of October 5, at approximately six o'clock.

Everyone went home to bed or off to Thanksgiving weekend.

During the fracas one of the new senators, John Lynch-Staunton of Quebec, had been persistently attempting to find out from me what was going to happen by asking whether he should phone his wife and tell her to start the Thanksgiving turkey or not.

He now knew as did many others, no doubt with the same concerns. The senators wouldn't be eating much turkey this Thanksgiving.

VIII
The Law Is Me and I Am the Law

How to get rid of this bozo?

O N THANKSGIVING DAY I joined a meeting with Senators MacEachen, Stewart and Fairbairn, all of us refreshed by sleep except perhaps Senator MacEachen who had flown back directly from Europe. Senators Stewart, Fairbairn and I reviewed for Senator MacEachen the bizarre events leading to the Thanksgiving adjournment.

We were particularly concerned about the jamming of the House of Commons rules on questions of privilege into our rules. The House of Commons rules give their *elected* Speaker a much larger role than the Senate rules gave to our *appointed* one. In this case the House of Commons procedure was being imposed upon the Senate rules despite the provisions of Rule 33, which clearly sets out what happens when a senator raises a point of privilege and leaves the decision to the Senate, not to the Speaker.[1]

We also discussed the actions in the 1950s of Speaker René Beaudoin of the House of Commons, when he tried to step in and take over proceedings by personally putting a proposal to the House. The result was the destruction of a promising parliamentary career, and the eventual defeat of the Liberal government in the next election. Such a solution was, of course, not available in 1990 with an unelected Senate.

We also discussed what strategies were available to us to defeat the GST now that we were in a numerical minority (providing the royal stackers were allowed to vote) and whether we could mount an organized filibuster, which would require months of effort.

A senator can speak only once when the Senate is debating a bill and only once on any amendment. This meant our group effort on the GST would also require heroically long individual efforts and that eventually the votes on the GST would have to take place. That's why we tried to delay ever getting to it before the end of 1990.

Senator MacEachen felt our problems all turned on the Speaker and the "gang of eight." The Speaker, he felt, was irreparably tainted and that we must consider the wording of a censure motion and the timing of such a motion. Should it be done on Tuesday, to make our position clear to the Senate and the public? Should we state then that the Opposition would do everything in its power to stop business, until the Speaker was replaced by someone who could be trusted to observe the rules?

Should we sit in the meantime on regular business? Should we agree to definite hours on the bill to claw back old-age security pensions and family allowance payments? Should we participate in a vote on any bill in which the gang of eight took part before their legitimacy had been settled?

Then on October 9, the day after Thanksgiving, at eleven in the morning, Senators MacEachen, Stewart, Fairbairn, Molgat, Kirby and I met in Senator MacEachen's office.

Senator John Stewart, a professor, former member of the House of Commons and expert in parliamentary procedure and constitutional history, focused our attention on Speaker Charbonneau and the importance of his position. If what the Speaker had done was allowed to become a precedent, so that votes could continue to be held contrary to the rules and in the absence of the Opposition, a complete breakdown of the parliamentary system could be expected, in Senator Stewart's view.

Our public-relations adviser recommended that the whole issue be broadened from parliamentary procedure to a general attack on the GST. Senators MacEachen and Fairbairn emphasized the need for linkage to the GST, but Senator MacEachen also reminded us we still faced a full-scale filibuster if the Speaker was prepared to do whatever the government wanted and was ready to ignore parliamentary procedure to get the GST through on behalf of the man who had appointed him as Speaker, Brian Mulroney.

Senator Molgat, the elected Deputy Speaker and chairman of the Rules Committee, felt that it was important to do something about the Speaker by way of motion to censure or otherwise. He also reminded us that before getting to the orders of the day there was provision in the rules for petitions. Senator Bill Petten said that there was evidence of very firm support for the fight against the GST in the country and certainly in our caucus, and that our people seemed to be ready to do everything that was necessary to fight the tax.

We decided we should continue the privilege attack on the Speaker until six o'clock on Tuesday, October 9. We would not let the Tories get to the item on the GST, and if we were thrown into a vote we would not leave the Senate chamber to permit the Tories to hold a vote in our absence.

At our caucus meeting at eleven that morning, there was much discussion of what Speaker Charbonneau had done. We were now convinced that the Speaker was prepared to do anything to achieve the Prime Minister's objectives. How could the Senate operate under such circumstances? What if there was another attempt to take a vote?

With our caucus colleagues we then walked through the plan discussed in Senator MacEachen's office that morning, our leader pointing out in summary that there was no way we could force Senator Charbonneau out of the chair.

Only Mr. Mulroney could do that.

But a motion of censure might hasten the Speaker's departure.

Notes

1. This word "privilege," as used about parliamentarians, is almost always, and understandably, misunderstood by others. It sounds like a claim for some lordly special status. It isn't. When applied to a parliamentarian, a breach of privilege is an interference with, or impediment to, the liberty to do his or her job. It arose in England when the king, impatient with the people's representatives' interference with his royal wishes, by, for example, refusing to impose a tax he wanted, would arrest them or otherwise prevent them from doing the job the people had sent them to Parliament to do. So Parliamentarians have always been very touchy about any king, or prime minister, or their servants, interfering with their "privilege" to do their jobs. Each house always has insisted on controlling the rules about how questions of privilege are dealt with.

IX

They Shoot Horses, Don't They?

Picture the Senators snug in their sleeping-bags.

O N OCTOBER 9, the day after Thanksgiving, the Senate resumed at two in the afternoon with Senator John Stewart on his feet raising a new question of privilege. Other senators joined in, all of them on the Liberal side.

We were now working in shifts to make sure that we were there with speakers planned and assigned around the clock.

We had organized ourselves into teams with a captain and whip for each team—our chief whip, Senator Petten of Newfoundland, serving as chairman of the team captain group.

We drew up elaborate schedules for the round-the-clock sittings we anticipated would continue.

Round-the-clock sittings were still possible in the Senate because closure and time allocation on speeches were not then possible under the Senate rules. Such sittings would not be allowed in the House of Commons.[1]

I stayed on until four in the morning and with assurance that the debate was continuing, went home for a bit of sleep. I slept until about ten that morning and then went back to the Senate.

The fire alarm had sounded about half an hour after I left, and the senators had stopped talking until about 6:30 a.m.

when it was cleared. Debate then continued on the privilege point and the filibuster resumed full flow.

At about twelve noon Senator Murray, the leader of the government, tried to justify the Speaker's lockout vote in the absence of the Opposition and said that the agreement he had made with me on the previous Friday had been broken because we were, in effect, filibustering.

I could see that this was just one of Senator Murray's attempts to justify his failure to control the Senate so long as he had to follow Senate rules. We heard he was having to explain several times a day to the Prime Minister, cabinet colleagues and the media why he couldn't use his new majority to have his way.

We never agreed to anything that would deter our plan to block the GST. In every discussion we made it clear we never would, just as Senator Murray made it clear he would never agree to anything that foreclosed the chance to have a vote to get the GST passed.

Senator MacEachen suggested that the Senate deal with other legislation and try to overcome the problem created by the Speaker's misconduct through negotiation. No way were we going to permit the Speaker's action in holding a vote on October 4 in the absence of the Opposition to be a precedent.

Debate continued on the question of privilege with many Liberal Senators taking their part.

By this time we had perfected our squad system. All Liberal senators were on one of four teams and continued to work in six-hour shifts on rotation.

This meant that when we established a strategy for speaking on privilege or whatever the team captains could divide the speaking responsibilities among team members for their shift period.

TEAMS

A

ADAMS
BOSA
CORBIN
CROLL
DEBARE
GIGANTES
HAIDASZ
HEBERT
LEBLANC, Fernand
MacEACHEN
PETTEN
STEWART, John
TURNER

B

BONNELL
DENIS
GRAHAM
HAYS
KIRBY
LEWIS
MARSDEN
OLSON
PERRAULT
ROBICHAUD
SPARROW
STEUART, D.G.

C

BUCKWOLD
DAVEY
FAIRBAIRN
FRITH
HASTINGS
KENNY
LEFEBVRE
MARCHAND
NEIMAN
RIEL
RIZZUTO
STOLLERY
VAN ROGGEN

D

AUSTIN
COOLS
GRAFSTEIN
KOLBER
LEBLANC, Romeo
LUCIER
MOLGAT
STANBURY
THERIAULT
THOMPSON
WATT
WOOD

ROTATION

Group	Time	Date
A	8 p.m. — 2 a.m.	Wednesday, Oct. 10/90
B	2 a.m. — 8 a.m.	Thursday, Oct. 11/90
C	8 a.m. — 2 p.m.	Thursday, Oct. 11/90
D	2 p.m. — 8 p.m.	Thursday, Oct. 11/90
B	8 p.m. — 2 a.m.	Thursday, Oct. 11/90
C	2 a.m. — 8 a.m.	Friday, Oct. 12/90
D	8 a.m. — 2 p.m.	Friday, Oct. 12/90
A	2 p.m. — 8 p.m.	Friday, Oct. 12/90
C	8 p.m. — 2 a.m.	Friday, Oct. 12/90
D	2 a.m. — 8 a.m.	Saturday, Oct. 13/90
A	8 a.m. — 2 p.m.	Saturday, Oct. 13/90
B	2 p.m. — 8 p.m.	Saturday, Oct. 13/90
D	8 p.m. — 2 a.m.	Saturday, Oct. 13/90
A	2 a.m. — 8 a.m.	Sunday, Oct. 14/90
B	8 a.m. — 2 p.m.	Sunday, Oct. 14/90
C	2 p.m. — 8 p.m.	Sunday, Oct. 14/90
A	8 p.m. — 2 a.m.	Sunday, Oct. 14/90
B	2 a.m. — 8 a.m.	Monday, Oct. 15/90
C	8 a.m. — 2 p.m.	Monday, Oct. 15/90
D	2 p.m. — 8 p.m.	Monday, Oct. 15/90
B	8 p.m. — 2 a.m.	Monday, Oct. 15/90
C	2 a.m. — 8 a.m.	Tuesday, Oct. 16/90
D	8 a.m. — 2 p.m.	Tuesday, Oct. 16/90
A	2 p.m. — 8 p.m.	Tuesday, Oct. 16/90
C	8 p.m. — 2 a.m.	Tuesday, Oct. 16/90
D	2 a.m. — 8 a.m.	Wednesday, Oct. 17/90
A	8 a.m. — 2 p.m.	Wednesday, Oct. 17/90
B	2 p.m. — 8 p.m.	Wednesday, Oct. 17/90

We also had meetings of the team captains regularly to avoid having to hold full caucuses to meet the many crises.

I was trying to spend time with each team, so I started by taking naps on a sleeping bag in my office.

Then I switched to a schedule of arriving at the Senate at about 5:00 a.m. to be with the first team of the day, and then going home about 8:30 p.m., just after the fourth team had started.

I would go to bed shortly thereafter, to be up in time to be with the next shift again at 5:00 a.m.

The exercise had some tiresome and tiring aspects, but I found it stimulating and invigorating. I didn't seem to have any difficulty getting by on little sleep as long as I didn't eat much or take any stimulants or depressants—no coffee, no tea and no alcohol.

This state of affairs continued until Thursday, October 11.

Technically, of course, the Senate was still in the sitting of Tuesday, October 9; consequently the Senate debates for the ninth had to be numbered A, B, C, D and so on, for what were in fact different calendar days.

By this time I think the Tories were realizing that we meant business.

They too were on a shift system, and were trying always to field enough senators to assure a quorum.[2]

We occasionally called quorum just to keep them on their toes, but there were always enough of them close by to come in to make up the difference.

I am told they had a room in the building set up with cots. I used a sleeping bag in my office to catnap, but I think most of our people went to their Ottawa hotel or other home when they were off shift and caught up on their sleep there.

Most of our people seemed to find the experience as invigorating as I did....

But it soon became apparent that although we could probably continue round the clock seven days a week for a while, we couldn't do it for months.

Something had to give.

Remember, the effective date of the legislation was January 1, 1991. We were convinced the government had to have it passed well before that date.

On Thursday, October 11, Senator Murray complained that forty-two hours of "debate on the whole question of privilege" was too much and urged the Speaker in effect to resort to House of Commons procedures permitting him to rule that he had heard enough.

But instead of asking for the ruling right then he bootlegged a motion that Orders 1, 2, 3 and 4 (the ones on other legislation ahead of the GST) be postponed so that the government could get to the GST.

Our people quickly objected and declared they were continuing on the question of privilege.

Senator Murray, of course, argued that he had made a motion.

Senator Gerald Ottenheimer, who was sitting in the chair, asked for a twenty-minute adjournment and left the chair.

Senator Molgat, the elected Deputy Speaker, stepped into it, with near-riotous consequences.

Shortly after noon the Senate adjourned because of some technical sound problems. It resumed about two o'clock in the afternoon when debate on the question of privilege continued.

And so it continued on into Friday, October 12.

Notes

1. The Tories unilaterally introduced closure and time allocation into the Senate rules in June 1991.
2. No business can be done in the Senate unless at least fifteen senators, including the Speaker, are present. If a lack of quorum is noted by a senator, the Senate must be adjourned unless a quorum can be quickly raised by bringing in senators from nearby rooms.

X
We, the People

The Tories get a little annoyed by the mountains of petitions.

THE RIGHT TO petition the Crown and Parliament is an ancient, long-established and fundamental principle. *Beauchesne,* the Canadian Parliament's procedural bible, states that in Canada "the right of petitioning the Crown and Parliament for redress of grievances is acknowledged as a fundamental principle of the Constitution and has been exercised without interruption since 1867."

The right was inherited at Canada's very beginning from the constitutional principles of England where, from early times, it has been exercised without interruption for centuries. It has had a profound effect in determining the main forms of parliamentary procedure. In England the power of Parliament to deal with petitions and the rights of petitioners was laid down in 1669.

And so at that point we shifted the filibuster tactic to the question of presenting petitions against the GST.

They were now starting to flow onto the desks of Liberal senators. Thousands and thousands of names from all across the country were accumulating. Senator MacEachen's office alone received tens of thousands of letters and names on petitions. Boxes of them are still, well into 1991, stacked in his office and he has been steadily writing letters of acknowledgement since March, 1991. His office also kept some records of telephone calls. On October 4, 1990, for example, it received 143 calls of support and only five in opposition. And as our stand against the GST became widely publicized, all Liberal senators began to be deluged with mail and telephone calls.

In retrospect it's hard to recapture or measure, and for anyone not on the scene to understand, the psychological effect of the daily tide of petitions, mail and telephone calls. Senators are not used to such public attention, certainly not attention that goes beyond simple support and becomes enthusiastic cheering.

The daily mail and telephone calls were not uniformly encouraging. Some were bitterly critical. But many showed an impressively thoughtful understanding of what was happening and what was at stake. Others didn't understand exactly what we were doing but their opposition to the tax was so fierce that they asked us to keep doing it anyway. In my own case the cheers outnumbered the jeers by about nine to one. The other one out of eight was either neutral or puzzled.

Some thirty-five or forty senators, still under the team system, presented petitions, and took their time about it, as the names of Canadians opposed to the GST from all across the country were read in the Senate. This went on all day and night into Saturday, October 13. There was a short break on Saturday for lunch between 12:30 and 1:30 and then the petitions continued on all afternoon, all night, and on into Sunday, again with only a recess for lunch.

All this was infuriating to the government supporters in the Senate. At the most unexpected hours of day or night

74

Tories would burst into violent displays of bad temper and frustration, but we stuck to our strategy and tactics, ploughing on with our round-the-clock team rotation reading these signed protests against the GST from all parts of Canada.

XI
Can We Talk?

If you guys shape up we will too.

SOMETHING WAS BEGINNING to give. Senator Duff Roblin, Senator Murray's Conservative predecessor as government leader in the Senate, had been talking to Senator MacEachen about the possibility of negotiating an agreement for a more civilized regime.

Why was the initiative taken by Senator Roblin rather than by Senators Murray or Doody, the government leader and deputy respectively? We were a bit mystified, but we were interested in anything that would make our filibuster more workable for the long haul, especially if it provided relief for weekends and some week nights.

Meetings started among Senators Roblin, Murray, MacEachen and myself.

On Sunday, October 14, after the six o'clock dinner break, the Senate resumed at eight and Senators Murray and MacEachen were able to announce that discussions attempting to solve some of the problems were under way. The sitting was suspended until Monday at two in the afternoon.

Here was the position of each side at this point.

We wanted to be sure that we could develop our tactics within the framework of the Senate rules. This meant no more outlaw strikes by the Speaker, and the expunging of any precedent flowing from what he had done on October 4 when he held that blatantly unfair vote in our absence.

The government supporters had endured over a hundred hours of round-the-clock filibuster, including the apparently endless reading of petitions, and no end was in sight. Their Senate leadership had not even come close to getting debate started on the GST bill or even on the Committee's killer report. In fact, they had not even got to the orders of the day, where the GST question stood at number 5, because, as we've seen, the reading of petitions comes on the order paper well before that point, and we had demonstrated that we had no intention of letting them get to orders of the day at all if we could prevent it.

The common starting ground for the Murray/Roblin and MacEachen/Frith discussion was votes, because we wanted to prevent the Speaker forcing votes, and they wanted to be sure we could not use endless bell-ringing as a part of our arsenal.

Well, the negotiations went on and on, usually in my office —probably the smallest one in the Senate and not as attention-getting for the media as the offices of Senators Murray or MacEachen.

Meanwhile, ex-Senator Jacques Flynn, a former Conservative government leader in the Senate, had been called in from retirement to advise the government and Tory senators (on a fee basis) about tactics and negotiations.

We hadn't gone very far in our meetings before we decided that Senators Murray and Roblin were not really prepared to agree to anything until it had been checked with and approved by Flynn and the Prime Minister's office. Each time we seemed to settle on a point it had to be sent to Senator Murray's office where, apparently, batteries of experts were gathered to huddle over every word. It was all very bizarre; like truce negotiations while the war went on. Since this seemed to be the biggest story in town, there soon was a battery of media folks waiting outside my office for news of developments.

When we resumed about two in the afternoon of October 15, Senator Murray tried to move that the Senate proceed to reading of orders of the day. That way he could open a detour around the reading of petitions and then to the little matter of the GST. But after another rumpus about the fact that his motion was out of order, we went back to reading petitions. At 4:30 p.m. the Speaker suspended the sitting and asked the two leaders to meet with him in his office. We resumed at about 6:00 p.m. and suspended until about two o'clock the next day.

I must explain at this point why the difference between adjourning the Senate and suspending a sitting became very important. Please bear with me.

If a sitting is suspended it resumes at exactly the point of the day's work at which it stood and under whatever heading was in effect when it was suspended. For example, if we are reading petitions when a sitting is suspended we commence with petitions again whenever the sitting resumes. But if the Senate adjourns, when it next sits it starts back at the top of the order paper which, of course, further pushes the government back from ever getting to its beloved GST. Accordingly the government always preferred suspension to adjourment, since they figured we'd eventually exhaust our mountainous piles of petitions.

By this time there seemed to be hope of some success in the negotiations, so by Tuesday, October 16, when we resumed at 6:00 p.m. we suspended immediately and then at nine o'clock that night we suspended again until two o'clock Wednesday afternoon to let the negotiations go on.

The government naturally wanted a definite date and time to begin debating the GST bill. But we couldn't give it to them because to do so would simply be tossing in the towel.

We finally settled on an agreement as to the length of bells for votes, and the option to postpone votes until a specified time. Also to permit adjournment motions for weekends and one night per week. There would be provisional rules accordingly—effective until after prorogation, that is until the next session of Parliament which would probably be in six or seven months.

The Tories saw this as a substantial gain.

So did we, because it meant an end to round-the-clock, seven-day-a-week sittings, and, equally important, it meant that all Senate rules were thereby reaffirmed except only as changed by these "provisional rules." Naive trust, as it turned out.

In addition to the provisional rules there was agreement on a legislative time table for certain other government legislation then before the Senate, namely the controversial "clawback," the Unemployment Insurance changes, Hibernia, and some other bills.

We also agreed on the number of amendments—eight—the Liberals could move to the GST bill, and about a time for the vote on each of those amendments. We agreed to this because there still were many procedural tactics available under the rules (reaffirmed by this agreement) as long as we insisted on no agreement for a final time of vote on the GST. And with the provisional rules we had, we thought, effectively "erased" the abomination of October 4, a vote with only one side participating.

On October 17, Senator Murray formally announced that finishing touches were being put on the legal drafting and that in the meantime the two sides had agreed to begin debate on the message from the House of Commons concerning our amendments to Bill C-28. This was the infamous clawback legislation under which the government pays out the old age security and Canada pension and then claws them right back in an amount, for many 100 per cent, based on taxable income. After the debate had begun, the sitting was again suspended, this time until the following day.

By then we were into typing the previous night's agreement while Senator Murray and Roblin were checking with their cabinet colleagues. At 6:30 p.m. the provisional rules agreement was introduced in the Senate by Senator MacEachen, and Senator Murray introduced the house order providing for the sequence in which we would deal with the specific government legislative program.

It was a time of feverish activity the likes of which, I am sure, the Senate has never seen and may never see again.

XII

An Uneasy Calm

The killer report gets killed....

FROM THIS POINT things settled down a bit. Under the Senate order the government was making progress on its legislative business. Not the GST, but other bills such as the Unemployment Insurance Bill.

On October 25 the adoption of the September 25 report of the Committee recommending the Goods and Services Tax be killed was defeated 57 to 51. All eight of the royal stackers voted against the report and thus for the tax. Without them the GST would have died, and the government would have had to start all over again in the House of Commons, and in a brand new session, in order to try to impose its Goods and Services Tax.

But only the Committee report had been dealt with. The GST legislation itself was still not passed and was a long way down the order paper agenda.

On October 30 we were back to petitions. Senator Doody, the government deputy leader, jumped us with a petition *in favour of* the GST. Phew! Where did he find anyone to sign a petition in favour of the GST? Well, his petition was signed by three members of Senator Murray's staff. I guess other supporters were hard to find. Senator Doody hoped to interrupt the Liberal senators reading their hundreds of names and to give the Speaker an excuse to recognize him, although a Liberal senator was speaking at the time. I am firmly convinced that it had all been worked out with the Speaker: he would recognize Senator Doody no matter what, to give him the floor under the heading of petitions. Otherwise, the Liberal senators would have continued reading petitions, those petitions with hundreds and hundreds of names that kept flowing in.

So after thousands of names presented to the Senate against the tax, there stood Senator Doody with a petition with only three names in support and all of them employees in Senator Murray's office. Oh yes, and the name of the president of the Canadian Manufacturers' Association which had been faxed in that day.

We had some fun with that.

All that effort to produce a total of four people in favour of the GST? Obviously, by giving Senator Doody the floor, the Speaker had allowed him to smuggle in a motion to jump forward to the GST on the orders of the day.

And Senator Doody, having been given the floor by the Speaker, did just that. He moved that the orders of the day be now read.

And away we went with another rumpus over whether this motion could be made while the Senate was busy under the heading of petitions. Further debate about whether the right to present petitions had been "prostituted" (Senator Murray's term) and Senator MacEachen's affirmation of the Opposition's right to delay—and on, and on, up until Thursday, November 1.

Another milestone.

We'd managed, against the Tory majority, to delay the tax right through October.

So why not November and then December?

Especially with the new and better hours.

XIII
The Amendments: No Times Eight!

This chapter alone is worth 7 per cent of the cost of this book.

THE GOVERNMENT HAD arrived at final installment debate on the GST. The first amendment on reading material was introduced by Senator MacEachen. We had very carefully worked out the subject and the order of the limited number of amendments agreed to.

The eight amendments were as follows:

1. Remove the tax from books and other reading materials.
2. Remove the tax from basic necessities such as electricity and home heating fuels.
3. Remove the tax from co-ops.
4. A cost-of-living adjustment in the goods and services tax credit and the level of income at which it applies, so that low-income families would be given some protection from inflation.
5. Fairer transitional relief measures for business and new home buyers which would reduce the risk of double taxation in the early stages of the GST.
6. Remove the tax from a wide range of educational services, health care services and funeral costs.
7. Remove the tax for Northerners who already pay double or triple the cost of goods and services in the south.
8. A higher tax on luxury items such as yachts, expensive

cars and jewellery in return for removing the tax on books, children's clothing and non-prescription drugs.

The Conservatives managed an almost complete turnout for every vote, whereas various of our members were sick in hospital and only two of the six Independent senators—Lawson and Waters—could be relied upon to vote with us.

While some of the Conservative senators agreed with some of our amendments, almost none of them rose to speak on any of them.

Conservative Senator Solange Chaput-Rolland was vehemently opposed to taxing books and reading. But she voted with the government against our amendment.

Tory Senator Claude Castonguay agreed that the transitional costs for business, especially the insurance industry, should be amended and he had the courage to abstain from voting.

But the eight contested Section 26 royal stacker senators were there and voted against every amendment every time. Had those eight additional senators not voted the amendments would have passed by a clear margin.

Speaker Charbonneau also voted on every amendment, and with the government.

Why the government failed to accept one or more of these very reasonable amendments, and thereby cut some of the political ground from under us, I will never understand. For example, if they had accepted the amendment on reading material, on the co-ops, on energy or a couple of others, I think some of the public opposition would at least have been mitigated. All these amendments had very strong and publicly active special-interest and general support.

As each amendment went down to defeat, I noted for the record that if the "British" Senators had not voted the amendment would have carried.

By this time we realized that the next crisis was going to relate to the right of the Independent senators to propose amendments. Why should they not be allowed to move amendments when the Liberals had been allowed eight?

They had not participated in the negotiations and therefore did not feel bound by any limit on the number of amendments.

If Senators Stan Waters, an Independent representing the Reform Party, and Ed Lawson, another Independent and president of an important workers union, both strongly opposed to the GST, could propose amendments, debate could continue for as long a time as our team system held up, and each of our fifty-three Liberal senators could speak at length on each amendment. Moreover, under the arrangement the Senate approved on October 18, we were no longer required to sit twenty-four hours a day, seven days a week.

So it all came down to what was going to happen after the last Liberal amendment had been dealt with.

Here's how the two sides lined up.

We wanted Senator Waters (who became ill and died as this book was in its final stages) to be recognized, and in due course Senator Lawson, to introduce amendments, so that debate could continue. This would add days and days to what we hoped would be a fatal delay of the GST. At their request we already had discussed possible amendments with the Independents, Senator Waters and Lawson, because they were not bound by the agreement about the number of and time for amendments.

This was all anticipated by the other side, of course. Senator Orville Phillips, the government whip, and Tory colleague Senator Bill Kelly had invited the two Independents (Waters and Lawson) to dinner at the Rideau Club to try to make some deal that would tie them down.[1]

What the government wanted was either to limit the number of amendments the Independents could put, or, if they were unable to achieve that, to move "the previous question" before Senators Waters or Lawson could get on their feet to move amendments.

The expression "previous question" simply means closure or a form of it. In effect it asks the Senate to decide that a vote shall be taken immediately on the question then before the Senate. The motion asking that the Senate so decide is debatable but cannot be amended. Once the motion for the "previous question" carried, the vote would have to be taken forthwith on the GST question. So, if the government could get "the previous question" motion moved, it could at least see some tunnel-end light, and know that that motion could not be amended, thereby starting another round of debate on the amendments. That's why it amounts to a form of closure.

And that's where things stood when the Liberals' last amendment on the GST was defeated on Thursday, November 22.

Both sides were on the edge of their seats—the Liberals wanting Senator Waters to be allowed to move a motion to amend the GST, enabling us to continue our filibuster, and the Tories wanting to get the floor to move the previous question to shut off all further amendment or debate on the GST and to limit the rest of the proceedings to debate on the previous question or closure motion.

Again it came down to the Speaker. What would happen when the last Liberal amendment was dealt with? Who would get the floor?

Senator Waters would be on his feet for sure, and Senator Murray, or someone on the government side, would be as well. Senator Waters with his amendment which would continue the delay, the government with its previous question motion to cut it down—whom would the Speaker recognize?

Obviously the government would want the Speaker to refuse to recognize Waters and to recognize someone on the Tory side.

Notes

1. Senator Waters was a member of the Reform Party, but "independent" of the two large parties, Liberal and Conservative.

XIV
Over to You Again, Guy

Do we detect a certain lack of fair play in the Senate?

B Y THIS TIME none of us doubted that the Speaker would try anything to help the government. He had voted with the government against all the amendments. Under Senate rules he was entitled to do so. The Speaker of the House of Commons is not so entitled, a further illustration of what an anomaly the Speaker's position is in the Senate. But while he is entitled to vote and speak on any issue he wishes, he does so as a senator and not as the Speaker.

That's why we were so sure that the Speaker would be prepared to do whatever he could to help the government by letting them move their motion for the previous question, thereby depriving Senator Waters of his right to propose amendments. Senator Waters, remember, was the first "elected" senator, so if the government was prepared to cut him off they were obviously prepared to risk a lot of political flack to ram through their unpopular tax.

Well, on Thursday, November 22, Senator Waters made an important move. He was presenting petitions and as he finished he told the Speaker he would be introducing an amendment after the Liberals' eighth amendment had been voted on. Thus notified well in advance that Waters wanted recognition immediately after that vote, Speaker

91

Charbonneau was in a corner. Rule 26 provided that the Speaker could recognize whomever he thought rose first but, as with all other matters, the Senate itself had the final decision. Any senator could then move that some other senator "be now heard" instead of the Speaker's choice, and that motion was to be decided by the Senate. With the Independents voting with us we could very well win such a vote, thereby in having Senator Waters present amendments which could then be debated to delay further a final vote on the GST, probably long enough to wreck government plans for the implementation of the tax.

So on Thursday, November 22, with the vote on the last of the Liberal amendments to be taken at 5:45 p.m., we knew that if the Speaker refused to recognize Senator Waters all hell would break loose. So we had taken the precaution of going to see the Black Rod (the Senate version of "sergeant at arms") about how he saw his role. He had been appointed after the desk banging and so-called "kazoo" events of October 5, and had made a comment to the media about his role in maintaining order if it happened again. He told us that in his view the senators were in charge within the "bar" of the Senate, that is within the Senate area enclosing the seats of the senators, and he felt that only interference from outside would compel him to intervene.

The vote on the last Liberal amendment started at 5:45, as scheduled. When it had been completed, just before six o'clock, Senators Waters, Murray, Molgat and I immediately jumped to our feet. Senator Murray pretended to have been recognized by the Speaker and kept trying to move the previous question (closure) as expected. Senator Waters proceeded to read aloud his lengthy amendment. Senator Molgat and I moved that the Senate decide to recognize Senator Waters. All hell did indeed break loose with senators congregated around the Speaker insisting that the rules of the Senate required him to recognize Senator Waters, especially with Waters having told him the day before he would be rising to move an amendment and that, in any event, he had to entertain the motion that Senator Waters be now heard, leaving it to the Senate to decide for itself according to Rule 26.

I believe it had been all set up in advance. Appallingly, Speaker Charbonneau completely ignored our insistence that he follow the rules, to the outrage of all the senators on our side and the outrage of the senators on the other side at our outrage. Eventually, the sitting was suspended.

Notes

1. Senator Stan Waters was elected in an election established by the Alberta Legislature. He couldn't be elected under the Constitution but his election by the people put sufficient pressure on the Prime Minister, as the sole power to appoint senators, to exercise that power in favour of Senator Waters. So although not directly elected to the Senate, Waters was constitutionally appointed by the Prime Minister and that appointment was clearly the result of pressure from an election process.

XV
Help!

Outside the big top....

T HE WAR MEANWHILE was waging on other fronts outside the Senate. We were still talking to the lawyers, Mr. Sexton and Mr. Danson and others, about the qualifications of the "British" senators.

Also a question had arisen about Senator Forrestall's property qualifications. His eligibility would affect more than Senator Forrestall himself, because if he was not qualified then quite probably the other seven would not be qualified.[1] Appointment of stackers under the Constitution had to be made in batches of four or eight, not seven, and if only seven were qualified then probably all the others would be disqualified.

Senator MacEachen had opened a third front by asking Liberal senators who were members of the Commonwealth Parliamentary Association to get that body interested in what we saw as clear breaches of parliamentary rules by Senator Charbonneau. Earlier, on a fourth front, a letter had been sent to the Governor General asking him not to exercise his power under Section 26. The Governor General's response was unhelpful.

Back to the uproar caused when the Speaker refused to recognize Senator Waters, and instead recognized the government leader, Senator Murray.

When we resumed about four o'clock in the afternoon on Friday, November 23, the Speaker reported that attempts were being made to resolve the impasse and at his suggestion the sitting of the Senate was suspended until the following Monday (November 26).

At this point we hoped we could win a vote that Senator Waters be recognized, because we expected that his fellow Independents might very well vote in his support, as we would, thereby overcoming the government's numbers.

We were wrong.

It turned out we could not count on any Independent except Senators Waters and Ed Lawson.

Senators Waters and Lawson finally agreed with the government to limit the number of their amendments, so when we resumed on Monday we couldn't do anything but support what Waters and Lawson had agreed to.

That reduced us to other tactics we felt were still available to us under the Senate rules, including the provisional rules. We still, perhaps naively, thought that the government and its supporters would have to follow those rules as long as we hung in and forced them to. After all, the only changes they had expected had been negotiated and put into the newly added provisional rules about votes.

We had fulfilled our part of the bargain by trading passage of some of their other legislation (the Clawback, the Unemployment Insurance, Hibernia, and so on) for the advantage we had gained to maintain our fight against the most important target—the GST. But with that in the bag and having their side of the bargain wrapped up, might they be tempted to weasel out of their end?

Well, at 8:00 p.m. on November 26, the following Monday, Senator Waters moved his amendment to delay the GST for one year. It took almost an hour to read it because of the number of clauses to be changed to bring about that result. Then at our request, the Speaker read the entire amendment and debate followed with the vote deferred, according to the provisional rules.

The next day, after Senator Waters' amendment had been defeated, we used our once-a-week overnight adjournment, so the Senate sitting was suspended until Wednesday, at two o'clock.

On Wednesday Senator Lawson introduced his amendment, requiring that excess GST revenue be used to pay down the national debt. Debate followed and the vote was again deferred according to the provisional rules.

On Thursday, the Senate having been *adjourned*, we started at the top of the order paper and finally Senator Lawson's amendment was defeated and the sitting was suspended to eight o'clock that evening.

Senator Murray, the government leader, made his motion for the previous question, and the Speaker put the question. I raised a point of order concerning the accuracy of the official record of Thursday, November 22, the key date when we saw the Speaker again serve the government's purposes by breaking the rules by refusing to recognize Senator Waters and by refusing to let the Senate decide who should speak. The Senate record did not accurately record the events, and in particular the timing. It was agreed that the clerk would investigate and report back through the Speaker.

At this point debate on the motion for the previous question began, meaning in effect potential end to the debate on the GST, because when debate on the previous question ended a vote could immediately be forced on the GST.

Notes

1. The Constitution provides that, as one of his qualifications, a senator must be "seised" of property within the province or division for which he was appointed. A Halifax newspaper had dug up the fact that Senator Forrestall had an interest in some property in Nova Scotia but, according to expert opinion from lawyers and a professor that they had consulted, he was probably not "seised" of the property in the technical or legal sense. Looking, as we always were, for any way to defeat the GST, including any way of disqualifying the "gang of eight," we jumped at this chance to disqualify one of them and thereby probably disqualifying them all since they had to be appointed as a group of four or eight.

XVI
Back to the Mattresses

The home stretch and a graceless coup de grâce.

WE WERE REALLY down to the last ditch because we now had to filibuster the previous question motion, at least until the end of December, so that the government could not put the GST mechanism into place in time for it to come into effect on January 1. Our strategy assumed that so long as there was doubt about whether the tax would take effect on January 1, there would be enough uncertainty to prevent it getting back on the rails because of the massive public opposition to it.

The Tories now had to face the conclusion that, based on the experience of October and November, we were willing, and probably able, to filibuster past that deadline.

The team system began again. We were "back to the mattresses" with senators preparing for long sittings. Senator Dick Stanbury had prepared a memorandum with detailed suggestions as to how to solve the problem of energy input, and Senators Jacques Hébert and Herb Sparrow looked after devices to cope with bladder output for four, six, eight, ten or however many hours one could last on one's feet.

For your interest (and potential use) Senator Stanbury's helpful hints for filibustering appear on the following page.

The teams were clearly ready for all-day and all-night effort.

THE SENATE OF CANADA **LE SÉNAT DU CANADA**

November 15, 1990

TO: ALL LIBERAL SENATORS

FROM: DICK STANBURY

We all know that fairly soon each of us is going to have to make at least one major speech. The word "major" may mean different things to each of us. To Phillippe Dean Gigantes it may mean 15 to 24 hours. To me it will depend on my voice, my legs and certain other physical limitations. However, if our filibuster is to be effective, each will need to try to speak for as many hours as possible. My purpose is to make some suggestions as to how we might prepare ourselves and keep ourselves comfortable during our own speeches.

The following have occurred to me:

1. Use the Committee Report, the Proceedings of the Committee and the Briefs of the witnesses to lengthen the text of your speech. Long quotes are quite relevant.

2. Put your text (and materials to be read) in easily readable form.

3. Do not waste energy on emoting **or** projecting. Speak quietly and slowly saving yourself for lengthy speaking.

4. Arrange some build up of your chair to allow you to be sitting while you appear to be standing.

5. Be prepared to ask long questions of other speakers to give the speaker a bit of a rest.

In preparation, be sure that you

1. drink no fluids for several hours before the speech

2. sip water sparingly during the speech

3. have available candies to suck or other means of lubricating your mouth and throat

4. dress comfortably

5. be well rested

If you have any other ideas, please let us all know.

The debate on the previous question guillotine was started by Senator Peter Bosa at ten o'clock on the evening of November 29 and continued right through the night.

When I arrived from Ottawa's cold, wet, dark streets at five in the morning I was told Senator Earl Hastings had taken over a few hours earlier at two and then had had what turned out to be minor heart attack, which was confirmed in an ironic twist by Dr. Wilbur Keon, the eminent heart surgeon, one of the Prime Minister's Tory "stackers" who happened to be on shift for his side. Senator Len Marchand then spoke, and Senator Gil Molgat continued on for eight-and-a-half hours. Senator Hébert spoke for eighteen hours and fifteen minutes, the last stretch of eleven hours and fifteen minutes non stop, carrying on until five o'clock the following afternoon, when, according to the provisional rules, the sitting was suspended until Monday.

And so on through Monday, December 3, opening our fourth month of successful resistance—with very long speeches, records being made and broken. Senator Joyce Fairbairn, for example, started just after noon on Tuesday, December 4, and went on until 6:25 the following morning.

That's a long time to be on one's feet, unable to leave the Senate chamber, though occasionally able to sit down because of questions we arranged to have asked during speeches to enable speakers to rest their feet for a few moments while considering the questions. Tory senators were unwittingly similarly helpful when occasionally they angrily interrupted for question or comment.

Senator John Stewart started at 6:25 a.m. and went on until 3:30 in the afternoon, with a relevant, well-researched and eloquent review of the Speaker's outrages. Then just before midnight Wednesday night, Senator Philippe Gigantès started and continued right through until the sitting was suspended at 5:45 the following afternoon, December 6.

When the Senate resumed on Friday morning at nine, Senator Gigantès was still at it, and at noon that day the sitting was suspended for the weekend.

We came back on Monday, December 10, when, after some tributes to Senator Henry Hicks, who had been tragically killed in an automobile accident very shortly after his retirement from the Senate, Senator Gigantès arose to continue his speech on the previous question, but immediately moved that the debate be adjourned.

The vote on this motion was deferred until 5:45 the following afternoon in accordance with the provisional rules and the Senate proceeded to deal with other items on the order paper.

During the round-the-clock filibuster Senator MacEachen and I had been continuing our contacts with Jean Chrétien's office, with the caucus and with the party leadership, and were receiving co-operation and encouragement from those colleagues.

All of us, and particularly Senator John Stewart, Senator MacEachen and I, and the group of team captains, were constantly trying to anticipate what moves the Tories could make to break the filibuster on the previous question/closure motion.

We had been hearing rumours about a letter addressed to the Speaker, asking him to intervene to end debate, to be signed by all the Tory senators. Of course, there is nothing permitting this in the rules, but by now we were sensitized to the Tories' continuing search for any device, no matter how bogus and improper, to offer to the Speaker so the GST legislation could be passed by hook or by crook before the end of December.

We were worried.

Sure enough, on Tuesday, December 11, even before the Speaker said the prayers and the doors were opened for the public, Tory Senator Kelly was on his feet raising a point of order—not dealing with the prayer which was the item on the order paper at that point, but on the right of the Senate to decide on the GST, and presented a letter to the Speaker signed by all the Tory senators, except the Speaker himself.

This caused yet another outburst of angry debate on whether Senator Kelly had any point of order, and even if he did whether he could raise it at that time. Any independent Speaker would have ruled him out of order.

There was no Senate precedent for it, it was unheard of and in parliamentary terms it was an abomination even in the House of Commons because it was asking Speaker Charbonneau to do exactly what Commons Speaker René Beaudoin had tried to do over thirty years earlier on a much more minor issue, something Beaudoin had done to his eventual ruination.

The Speaker is not there to put questions before the Senate of his own motion. Questions are proposed by members of the Senate from the floor and the Speaker simply asks for the decision of the senators about them. He does not make motions from the chair, but that is exactly what Senator Kelly was asking Speaker Charbonneau to do.

After some debate Senator MacEachen moved that the Senate adjourn.

The Speaker arbitrarily ruled MacEachen's motion out of order. We appealed the ruling and the vote on it was deferred to 3:40 a.m. in accordance with the applicable provisional rule.

The sitting was then suspended.

But when the sitting was resumed by agreement at 5:45 p.m. (rather than 3:40 a.m.) the next day and the vote taken on Senator Gigantès' motion to adjourn the debate, Senator

Gigantès' motion was, as expected, defeated and we therefore withdrew the appeal on the Speaker's ruling.

The sitting was suspended until Wednesday, November 12.

That day, with Senators MacEachen and Waters both on their feet to speak on Senator Kelly's request that the Speaker impose a vote on the Senate, Senator Ed Lawson moved that Senator Waters now be heard under the applicable rule, Rule 26.

Debate followed, and the sitting was suspended at six o'clock. When it resumed as usual at eight the Speaker, ignoring all objections, presented his ruling on Senator Kelly's request. Although his ruling was not appealed he nevertheless acted as if it had and asked that senators be called in to vote on his ruling.

In the meantime Senator Stanbury had risen on a question of privilege. Senator Orville Phillips, the government whip, requested that the vote on the Speaker's ruling be deferred. The Speaker left the chair and the sitting was suspended.

The next morning we resumed at 8:45, with Senator Stanbury rising on the question of privilege and moving a motion of censure against the Speaker. Debate followed through until 5:45 p.m. when the votes began.[1] Senator Murray's motion for the previous question, in effect closure and forcing the GST vote, was carried, 54 to 50. Again in the absence of the royal stackers the motion for closure would have been defeated 50 to 46 and the GST itself would have been defeated.

But the stackers were present, they did vote and the GST wasn't defeated.

Then the GST vote itself was taken. It carried, again only because of the help of the stackers.

So back to our original question. How did the GST get passed?

That's how.[2]

Hail Charbonneau! If he had enforced, instead of broken, Senate rules, the GST would not have passed.

Here's why I think Speaker Charbonneau is entitled to so much credit for this back-breaking tax:

Without him the committee report killing the tax would have been adopted before the arrival of the royal stackers and the GST would have been killed as early as the week of September 24.

Without him no votes could have been taken in the absence of the Opposition.

Without his jackbooting the Senate rules on questions of privilege and applying House of Commons rules to the Senate, Senate rules could have frustrated the tax to death and we wouldn't be paying it today.

Without his ignoring an agreement approved by the Senate in early October about Senate order of business, he could not have forced "qualification" of the stackers to be recorded.

Without his allowing the stackers to vote while their right to do so was being questioned in the Senate and in the courts, the government would have lost all votes on the GST.

Without his refusal to allow the Senate itself to decide who should speak, as provided in the rules, two Independent senators could have exercised their rights and the GST would have been defeated.

Without his taking power and rights away from senators to put his own motions forward and call for votes, the GST vote would probably never have been taken—certainly not before the crucial date of January 1.

The government and the lonely few supporting the tax should give him a medal.

But does it matter?

There has been no outcry from the media, really none from the political scientists, very little from parliamentarians. Many seem to find procedural outrages in the Canadian Senate as having nothing to do with the rule of law or as being important to our political system. They seem to be found merely amusing.

Still there are some who think that it does matter, and *will* matter a lot for the parliamentary system.

Just this spring (1991) the government again has used closure to force the House of Commons to accept even more muzzling by changing its rules. The House continues to be reduced to little more than a tool of the Prime Minister and his cabinet, leaving the government unchecked by anything except a Senate, whose rules that same government, with, as I've tried to show, Speaker Charbonneau's indispensable help, was able contemptuously to disregard to get the GST through.

And it is now changing even those rules so it won't need Senator Charbonneau or any other Speaker the next time.[3]

Does it matter politically?

Perhaps not.

It's been said that an unpopular or even disgraced government's best friend is our short memory.

But maybe that will be our final and winning weapon— implacable remembering, remembering every one of the millions of times every day the cash register rings up another 7 per cent. And telling politicians, journalists, and any one who will listen (forget Mulroney) that we haven't quietly swallowed this outrage, but are damned mad and won't take it.

Notes

1. See the appendix for selections from the text of Senator Stanbury's blistering case against the Speaker.
2. That is, that's how it got through the Senate. Even after passage through the House of Commons and Senate, all laws must be approved by Parliament's third element, the Queen, by royal assent. That's done in the Senate chamber by either the Queen, the Governor General or a deputy (one of the Supreme Court of Canada judges) where a quorum of senators and a delegation of House of Commons members attend in an ancient ceremony to witness the granting of the royal nod. It's always been just routine but Senator Bud Olson was so incensed at the way the government had rammed the bill through the Senate that he felt it his duty as a privy councillor to tell the Governor General's representative about the outrage. We Liberals knew he was going to do it but didn't anticipate the result of his doing so. For the GST the ceremony took place on a Friday and by the time Senator Olson and others were through regaling the Governor General's deputy (Justice John Sopinka of the Supreme Court of Canada) the government leadership on the House of Commons side had let the House of Commons adjourn for the weekend so that there were no members available to answer the call to attend in the Senate chamber. So the whole ceremony had to be put off until the following Monday. Even with routine proceedings such as this the leader of the government in the Senate and his gang that couldn't shoot straight cocked it up, and this time there was no rule they could break to help them out.
3. Read on....

XVII
Rest in Peace

Senate bugler plays Last Post for democracy....

IN JUNE OF 1991 the emasculating surgery was completed. The House of Commons had already been taken care of by further amendments to its rules. No worry about effective opposition there.

Now the Senate, having shown what was possible under its rules by its fight against the GST, had to be taken care of.

In May, as soon as the new session started, Tory senators produced a fully baked package of rule changes. They had developed it in their own caucus without any outside consultation, and meant to slam it through to eliminate any future opposition to the government in the Senate.

They did so by usurping a majority on the committee of selection, the structure in the Senate for establishing membership on committees in the new sitting. These committees are supposed to reflect the standing in the Senate. The Tories do not have a majority in the Senate, but they grabbed a majority on this committee of selection because of their government position and then proceeded to give themselves a majority on all other committees—most importantly on the Rules and Orders Committee.

The Liberals protested that the Tories had no right to take this majority position.

The Liberals also protested that rule changes, even the draconian ones imposed in the House of Commons, at least started with consultation, and didn't come in fully baked from one of the caucuses. Proposals for such rule changes always at least *start* on a non-partisan basis.

Anyway, the Tories insisted they would be glad to have Liberal senators on their committee, provided the majority was a Tory one so that they could have their way no matter what.

The Opposition refused, so the committee, made up only of Tories, had no trouble getting the package through. The rules were adopted on June 18, 1991, by a majority vote in the Senate with the Tories using their superior numbers, including the royal stackers, to establish a new set of rules.

These new rules hand the keys of the Senate to the government. Total control of agenda and proceedings is in the hands of the government, which makes the Senate, like the House of Commons, a reliable rubber stamp for whatever the government wants.

The only effective opposition left to the government is the media, and perhaps academia, but neither of them seems to have noticed. Or if they have, they don't care.

Parliament can still play in its government-controlled playpen.

Otherwise, rest in peace.

Epilogue

A few ideas for Senate reform....

THAT'S HOW THE Parliamentary system has evolved (or degenerated) in Canada. The result is very satisfactory—for the government. A combination of amending, then breaking, then amending parliamentary rules has effectively silenced both Houses—because a government no longer can be forced to listen to the people's representatives *or* the people.

And apparently the people don't like that—at least not the part about them. They shouted their fury at the government from all the mail, telephone calls and petitions that piled up in Liberal senators' offices during the GST battle. Polls since have verified the same frustration. When the government decided to spend $25 million on a giant ear (Dr. Keith Spicer's "Citizens' Forum on Canada's Future") the people almost deafened it with the same message.

"You haven't listened. You're not listening and we don't believe you will listen, so when you fiddle with the Constitution this time, we want to be there (in a Constituent Assembly) to guarantee you do listen!"

The government, now deeply addicted to its bad habits, says: "Don't worry. We politicians will look after this. Trust us. We'll send a committee of politicians around to talk to you."

The constitutional exigencies may be coming to a head too fast for that. Genuine, long-overdue reform does seem possible, though it took a whack over the head by a two-by-four in the form of the Quebec separation threat to get our attention.

Certainly Senate reform has never seemed more possible. And I have a suggestion about that.

As a part of any institutional reform we could have a Senate that could force the government to *listen.*

First, it would have to be elected—otherwise it wouldn't have the political muscle to exercise whatever powers it was given. That has been the problem with the present Senate from the beginning—plenty of legal and constitutional power, but no political courage to exercise it because it wasn't elected.

So, elected?

Absolutely.

But how?

Remembering that the objective is to make the government listen to the peoples' concerns, including regional ones, it should not be elected in a way that would permit the government to control it and thus have the ability to continue not to have to listen to it.

And there is a way to ensure a Senate free of government control. Election by proportional representation almost never produces a majority, as one can see in the examples of, say, Israel and Italy. That can cause problems when the government stands or falls on support of several minorities. But we could have a Canadian Senate that couldn't throw the government out but could defeat its legislation. The government then would have to listen to the shifting regional or issue coalitions in the Senate and come up with compromises. The government would be unable to ram its way through uncompromisingly and mulishly by laying on majority party whips because it wouldn't have a majority.[1]

Further, to avoid government control by making the Senate a duplicate of the House of Commons, election should be for a fixed term, not coinciding with House of Commons elections except perhaps by occasional accident.

With such a Senate many controversial plans would never have passed in their original form: the National Energy Program, for instance, the drug patent legislation, the unemployment insurance reductions—and the GST.

Many corollaries flow from these propositions, and there's plenty of flexibility in implementation so long as the essential principle remains—an Upper House the government has to listen to and deal with because it doesn't dominate and ultimately control it.

Here are some corollaries:

1. The establishment of an electoral commission to set out senatorial regions. It would operate very much like the Electoral Boundaries Commission that sets up ridings or constituencies for the House of Commons. For the Senate such regions should be based on a sense of community and a sense of belonging rather than by representation by population. The obvious ones are the five big regions: Atlantic, Quebec, Ontario, Prairie and Pacific. But a case could be made for more and somewhat smaller regions, for example Nova Scotia's Sidney Hicks' proposed twelve with six senators per region: British Columbia, Alberta, Saskatchewan, Manitoba, Northern and Eastern Ontario, Southwestern Ontario, Western Quebec, Eastern Quebec, New Brunswick, Nova Scotia, Prince Edward Island, Newfoundland and Labrador. The very large cities (Toronto, Montreal, Vancouver) could be separate regions. Whether they coincide with provincial boundaries or not,

the important point is that the senators express a regional interest in national affairs, not the institutional and political interests of provincial governments. The equality of representatives should be by region—not by province. This would finesse the most difficult of the Triple-E (equal, elected and effective) propositions for Senate reform. Elected and effective are quite straightforward, but the debate on "equal" could go on forever, and why bother because it will never happen. Larger provinces will simply not agree to equal representation for the smaller ones.

2. The election should be for a fixed term. I suggest that half the Senate should be elected for each period. The six-year term in the United States with elections every two years for one-third of the senators tends to produce too-frequent elections. I prefer a ten-year term with elections every five years for each half. But there is no need to be adamant on that any more than on the exact composition of the regions.

3. The elections therefore would not be simultaneous with the election for the House of Commons. That could happen but only by coincidence when an election for the House of Commons was brought about by a dissolution at the same time as a senatorial election was taking place.

4. You would have to choose the precise system of proportional representation. There are many. The one that is immediately attractive has been working in Australia for forty years (the Senate in Australia was elected on proportional representation first in 1949). An Australian model is initially attractive because Australia shares a good deal in common with Canada, including constitutional origins, size, federal organization and so on. Applying any proportional representation system to Canadian voting experience says

that a Senate so elected would probably consist of coast-to-coast representation from the big three political parties, as long as they remain natural outgrowths of political reality in Canada: the Progressive Conservative party, the New Democratic party and the Liberal party. Maybe the Reform party, if it ever becomes national. Also there would probably be some representation from regional parties: perhaps a Western party and, as Tom Kent has suggested, a Maritime Alliance party. There could easily be some Quebec separatists or separatists from any other province for that matter, some Social Creditors and some others, possibly even some splinter groups such as the Rhinoceros party. That sort of diversity is the probable result of the proportional representation system which is desirable in a second chamber precisely because it means that political realities can find expression in a national forum—a forum they are shut out of by the present winner-take-all system.

5. Such a new Canadian Senate should not have the power to refuse supply (the money the government needs to operate each year) or directly to defeat the government. To refuse supply is the equivalent of defeating the government because it cannot operate without money. The Senate should have a limited veto on supply, maybe a month or two, but an absolute veto on all other legislation including tax legislation.

6. When, as will be rare, there is a genuine deadlock between the House and the Senate there can be conferences or even joint sittings, a device used in Australia to prevent a second double dissolution on the same measure. It's favoured by Senator Duff Roblin, who also favours an elected Senate.

7. The party system will continue to exist but will be modified in its application in the Senate by denying autocratic power to any one party in the Senate.

8. There should be no cabinet ministers in the Senate, except one government spokesperson. There are cabinet ministers in Australia's Senate, but even there, purists believe that the Senate's role as a check or balance is compromised by their presence in the Senate.

Those are some of the corollaries and attendant problems. None, it seems to me, are fatal to the desirable objective—a chamber of sober second thought representing regional and minority issues that the government must *listen* to.

It will only solve some of our problems and won't solve even those perfectly. But we are still not arguing that such a democratic process is streamlined, efficient or perfect—just the best yet devised, and surely a lot better than the one we've now got.

Notes

1. The Senate's new gag rules wouldn't be a problem either, because such a Senate wouldn't put up with them. It would remove the gags and elect a neutral Speaker. And the government, with no majority control, couldn't apply the gags to eliminate opposition.

Appendix

Appendix

DEBATES OF THE SENATE, December 11, 1990. Hon. Richard J. Stanbury: Honourable senators, I rise on a question of privilege. The Speaker has given a ruling that is a nullity. There was no proper point of order and the alleged ruling was without foundation under the rules and procedures of the Senate of Canada.

My point of personal privilege affects not only my privileges as a member of long standing of the Senate of Canada but the privileges of the Senate as a whole, and of each individual senator sitting anywhere in this chamber. The government bulldozer must be stopped before it destroys not only the Senate but the Parliament of Canada.

MOTION OF CENSURE
As a result, I find it necessary, sadly, to move, pursuant to Rule 33 of the *Rules of the Senate of Canada,* as follows:

> Whereas Speaker Guy Charbonneau, on September 27, 1990, left the Chair and ordered the doors locked although a sitting of the Senate was still in progress; and

> Whereas Speaker Guy Charbonneau, on October 4, 1990, broke the rules of the Senate by arrogating to himself the right to set the time for division in direct contravention of the *Rules of the Senate,* which provide that a vote will be taken only on the consent of the Whips; and

> Whereas the aforesaid violation of the *Rules of the Senate* was deliberate, as stated by Senator Charbonneau in a letter sent by him that day to four senators, with copies to six others; and

> Whereas Speaker Charbonneau aggravated his offence by not informing other senators of his intention to conduct the division on the question then before the Senate at 5:30 p.m. on October 4, 1990;

and

Whereas Speaker Charbonneau ordered the doors of the Senate chamber locked before the hour specified by himself in the aforesaid letter; and

Whereas by conducting the division on October 4, 1990 before the time specified in the aforesaid letter, Senator Guy Charbonneau — even assuming that he had the right to set the time of divisions — which assumption is false — violated section 17 of the *Constitution Act, 1867,* in that he supplanted the Senate of Canada by a clandestine assembly; and

Whereas Speaker Charbonneau collaborated with Government supporters to deprive other senators of their rights as senators, as suggested by the statement of Senator P. Michael Pitfield on October 9, 1990 ; and

Whereas Speaker Charbonneau, on October 30, 1990, interrupted a senator, a senator then presenting a petition, and gave the floor to another senator who, having presented two petitions — one from three members of Senator Murray's staff — moved that "the Orders of the Day be read now"; and

Whereas Speaker Charbonneau, on October 30, 1990, ruled that the motion— that the Orders of the Day be read now— which is defined by *Beauchesne* as a dilatory motion, can be used to set aside Rule 19 of the Senate; and

Whereas Speaker Charbonneau persisted in attempting to originate a new proceeding — by attempting to allow Senator Lowell Murray to move "that the original question be now put" — at an hour when, under Rule 12, a sitting of the Senate is suspended; and

Whereas Speaker Charbonneau persisted in attempting to allow Senator Murray to move "that the original motion be now put" at a time when, because the Orders of the Day had not been reached, that motion could not be received by the Speaker; and

Whereas Speaker Charbonneau conspired with supporters of the Government to deprive the Senate of its right, under Rule 26, to decide whether or not to hear an independent senator, Senator Stan

Waters, who had given notice of his wish to be heard.

And whereas he then acted as the negotiator on behalf of the Government with the two Independent Senators to come to the terms of an agreement under which Senator Waters and Senator Lawson would be allowed to propose amendments.

And whereas Senator Guy Charbonneau has now made a ruling contrary to the Rules and practices of the Senate curtailing the debate on the motion to move the original question on the Third Reading of Bill C-62.

And whereas Speaker Charbonneau has just now conducted an illegal vote of this assembly;

I move, seconded by the Honourable Joyce Fairbairn, pursuant to Rule 33 of the *Rules of the Senate,*

THAT, the privileges of Honourable Senators having been consistently abused by the Speaker of the Senate, the Senate do advise the Prime Minister that Senator Guy Charbonneau is unfit to continue to be the Speaker of the Senate.

. . .

Honourable senators, it is with great sadness that I move this motion, even though the necessity for it is born of personal shock and frustration at the loss of my personal privilege after 23 years in the Senate, and a sense of shame that honourable senators have allowed our institution to be so badly abused.

My complaint concerning the behaviour of Senator Guy Charbonneau is that he allowed himself to become the tool of a vindictive and dictatorial Prime Minister. Mr. Mulroney has no more regard for the preservation of the integrity of his friends and servants than he has for the democratic constitutional institutions of our country.

The Honourable Guy Charbonneau came to this Chamber in 1979 with a fine reputation as a soldier and businessman. He perpetuated that reputation throughout his service as Speaker of the Senate after his appointment to that post by the Prime Minister in 1984. It is only within the last few months that he has allowed his warm friendship and blind loyalty to Prime Minister Mulroney to cause him to abuse his honoured position as Speaker of this chamber.

His abuse of the rights and privileges of honourable senators has brought the Senate to an impasse and to the brink of chaos and collapse, as we have seen this morning. Unhappily, his blind loyalty to the Prime Minister was exacerbated by his lack of knowledge and understanding of the history and tradition of the Senate, and his lack of knowledge of, and respect for, the *Rules of the Senate.*

In an effort to avoid this final impasse, Senators Fairbairn, Lefebvre, Kirby and I visited the Speaker in his chambers after his offensive behaviour of November 22 and before the present debate began. Our purpose was to ascertain whether he intended to attempt any other manoeuvre, such as this one, to cut off debate on Senator Murray's improperly accepted motion on the previous question. In the course of our discussion, Senator Charbonneau expressed surprise that we should be upset by his previous breaches of the rules and his attempts to make new rules by precedent.

He expressed complete contempt for the present rules, and said that the whole book should be thrown out.

He said that, after this experience was over, we would have to write new rules. He also advised us that, before these events began in September, he had little knowledge of the rules but had learned a lot since. He offered the comment that he had not read *Beauchesne* and did not really know much about it until someone had referred him to a passage in it after he had refused Senator Molgat's motion ... under Rule 26 asking him to recognize Senator Waters. Senator Charbonneau told us of his personal, strong, partisan support for the GST and made no apologies for voting with the government on all of the amendments, although other Speakers have not voted since 1943. He also talked about how long the debate would go on in relationship to the need of the government to get the cheques out. We made it clear that getting the cheques out and the length of debate were not his concern as Speaker.

On being pressed by us as to whether he recognized the right of each speaker to speak once on the previous question motion, and to speak at length to make use of delay as a legitimate tactic of the opposition, he said he was aware of the rule that each senator could speak once and he knew of no rule which could limit the time of debate. Yet here we are; he is willing to entertain, and has entertained, a supposed point of order of

Senator Kelly, which is clearly out of order, and has now conducted an illegal vote on that matter.

[Eds. Note: *Stanbury continues with a review of the history and powers of the institution of the Speaker of the Senate and a review of recent events in the Senate.*]

Senator Charbonneau ... knows that, as a partisan appointee, appointed by the Prime Minister and permitted to speak in partisan debate and vote in partisan votes, his only claim to credibility and objectivity is his even-handed application of the rules of the Senate. He knows that the principle task of any Speaker of any legislative body is the protection of the rights of the minority and of the individual members of that body. He knows today what we know, and that is that he has allowed his office to be prostituted before the blandishments of a close friend, the needs of a desperate government and his own partisan desire to see a piece of legislation, even a bad piece of legislation, passed into law. Knowing all of that, he has made a ruling which is a nullity.

There is no proper point of order and the alleged ruling was without foundation in the rules and practices of the Senate of Canada. That ruling attempted to invoke closure in the Senate of Canada and now, by an illegal vote and illegal procedure, he has apparently obtained a vote which does exactly that.

Can you imagine what an eruption all of this would have caused in the country if it had happened in the House of Commons? Can you imagine the press reports? This is just the Senate, which has earned a reputation for not taking strong stands on behalf of the people of Canada. However, the Senate is important, especially so in circumstances where a failed government jams a bad bill through the House of Commons and the Senate becomes the only refuge of a worried and unhappy people.

[Eds. Note: *Stanbury continues with a discussion of a similar situation in the House of Commons in 1956, which led to the defeat of the Saint-Laurent government in the next election.*]

... The House of Commons and the Senate are fundamentally different institutions. As it is arguable as to whether closure or time allocation are appropriate in the House of Commons, it is beside the point here in the Senate today. The rules are quite clear. It is my privilege as a senator to address any piece of legislation that comes before this chamber and to air all my arguments, regardless of the time it takes to do so.... I need not remind Honourable Senators that we constitute the great majority of the opposition in this place, and that we are no small fraction of a minority. Our numbers in this chamber warrant respect. Our support outside the chamber cannot be ignored. We are legitimately representing the concerns of the vast majority of Canadian people and we do not want this bill to pass through Parliament.

The House of Commons, for their own reasons, has brought in rules of closure and time allocation. These rules do not exist in this place and they are, in fact, in direct contravention of the rules that are in place and that have hitherto been respected and obeyed. The government is able to cut off a debate at every opportunity in the House of Commons, but it has no right to do so here. The rules are crystal clear in this regard and there are no precedents that would justify action to the contrary. Let me repeat, there are no precedents that would justify action to the contrary.

Rule 30 specifies that it is the duty of the Speaker to ensure that every senator wishing to speak has the opportunity to do so before the final reply. Why in the world has the Speaker made no attempt to follow Rule 30? In addition, convention has dictated that senators do not have a time limit of any kind and, indeed, there is no instance where senators have been prevented from speaking as long as they deemed necessary. Thus there are no means, *de jure* or *defacto,* at the disposal of the government or the Speaker to limit debate here in any way. There are no means through law or convention to deny my rights and privileges as a member of the Senate to speak until I have thought fit to conclude my argument and made my case, and I personally have not yet spoken in the debate on Bill C-62.

In conclusion, honourable senators, there has been a deliberate circumvention of the rules and accepted practices in this place. The Speaker cannot have it both ways. He cannot take on the role of a judicial and arbitrary figure and still conduct himself as a servant of the government and bend to their every whim. Convention over the last 30 or 40 years has dictated that the Speaker does not act as an active partisan, relinquishing his right to vote or speak in the Senate. The Speaker cannot exercise his influence based on the respect of other senators while acting as an unabashed instrument of the government. Therefore, much to my personal regret, I suggest that it is in the interests of each member of the Senate of Canada and of the institution of the Senate of Canada that Senator Charbonneau cease to act as its Speaker. That is the only way in which our rights and privileges may be restored.

I would remind those on the other side that at some time in the future it may be important that their rights and privileges be respected by a future Speaker in this house. I would only add that I do not believe that a vote on this motion, decided by a partisan government majority in this chamber, can in any way resolve the difficulties into which the government and the Speaker have led us.

ROYCE FRITH was appointed to the Senate in 1977 by Pierre Trudeau. He served as Deputy Government Leader from 1980 to 1984 and Deputy Leader of the Opposition from 1984 to 1991. He was appointed Leader of the Opposition by Jean Chrétien in September 1991. A retired lawyer, Frith attended University of Toronto Law School, Osgoode Hall Law School, and the University of Ottawa. He was president of the Ontario Liberal Association, a member of the York County Council, Legal Advisor to the Commissioner of Official Languages, and a member of the Royal Commission on Bilingualism and Biculturalism. Frith was born in Montreal and lives in Ottawa.

Editors for the Press:
David McFadden and Sarah Sheard

Cover Design: Louis Fischauf/Reactor

Cover Illustration: Terry Mosher

Coach House Press
401 (rear) Huron Street
Toronto, Canada M5S 2G5

Printed in Canada